VICTORIAN CRITICAL INTERVENTIONS
Donald E. Hall, Series Editor

Educating Seeta

The Anglo-Indian Family Romance
and the Poetics of Indirect Rule

❖

Shuchi Kapila

THE OHIO STATE UNIVERSITY PRESS
Columbus

Copyright © 2010 by The Ohio State University.
All rights reserved.

Library of Congress Cataloging-in-Publication Data
Kapila, Shuchi, 1964–
 Educating Seeta : the Anglo-Indian family romance and the poetics of indirect rule / Shuchi Kapila.
   p. cm. — (Victorian critical interventions)
 Includes bibliographical references and index.
 ISBN-13: 978-0-8142-1126-7 (cloth : alk. paper)
 ISBN-10: 0-8142-1126-7 (cloth : alk. paper)
 ISBN-13: 978-0-8142-9224-2 (cd)
  1. Anglo-Indian literature—19th century—History and criticism. 2. Domestic fiction, English—19th century—History and criticism. 3. Indian women in literature. 4. Interracial marriage in literature. 5. Gardner, William Linneaus, d. 1833—Criticism and interpretation. 6. Croker, B. M. (Bithia Mary), d. 1920—Criticism and interpretation. 7. Taylor, Meadows, 1808–1876—Criticism and interpretation. I. Title. II. Series: Victorian critical interventions.
 PR9489.5.K37 2010
 823'.80935854035—dc22
                                      2009052643

This book is available in the following editions:
Cloth (ISBN 978-0-8142-1126-7)
CD-ROM (ISBN 978-0-8142-9224-2)
Paper (ISBN: 978-0-8142-5653-4)
Cover design by Janna Thompson-Chordas
Type set in Adobe Palatino, by Juliet Williams

CONTENTS

Acknowledgments • VII

Introduction
The Poetics and Politics of Anglo-Indian Romance • 1

PART I
Of Bibis and Begums: Company Affairs in Colonial India • 23

Chapter One
"Half an Asiatic": William Linnaeus Gardner and
Anglo-Muslim Domesticity • 33

Chapter Two
The Home and the Bazaar:
The Anglo-Indian Novels of Bithia Mary Croker • 52

PART II
Indirect Rule and the Politics of Romance • 79

Chapter Three
Family Quarrels: The Royal Widows and
the East India Company • 86

Chapter Four
Educating Seeta: Philip Meadows Taylor's
Romances of Empire • 108

Conclusion
Why Romance Matters • 128

Notes • 135
Bibliography • 148
Index • 158

ACKNOWLEDGMENTS

One of the greatest pleasures of finishing this book is in acknowledging the many intellectual and personal debts I have incurred in the too many years it took to complete it. This book began as a dissertation in the English department at Cornell University, where Biodun Jeyifo, Dorothy Mermin, Laura Brown, Paul Sawyer, and Harry Shaw shepherded it on its way with their generous readings and encouraging comments. A wonderful community of graduate students helped me flesh out this project. For their comments on early drafts of this work, I thank Elizabeth Davey, Charlene Gima, Dionne Espinoza, Laura Murray, Anna Neill, Paula Moya, Shalini Puri, and Talia Schaffer. Sarah Mckibben read parts of the manuscript, shared the pangs of completing graduate school, and has stayed a close friend ever since.

My years at Kenyon College helped me present work from the book and expand my research for its historical chapters. Wendy Singer and David Lynn became not only admired colleagues and friends but my extended family in Ohio. For her continuing engagement with my work and for teaching me all about the modern India I grew up in, I thank Wendy Singer. Kenyon College provided me with summer grants to pursue this research and the library staff gave expert research assistance. At the Institute for Research on Women at Rutgers University in 2000–2001, I benefited from the generosity and kindness of its director, Bonnie Smith. Ana Mariella Bacigalupo, Ethel Brooks, Christina Ewig and Robin Greeley—all at IRW that year—provided constant encouragement and excellent comments. Carolyn Vallenga Berman read and commented on chapters of the book.

Grinnell College grants enabled me to complete research on this book at the British Museum and Library and the National Army Museum in London. The staff of Burling Library, especially Richard Fyffe, Phil Jones, Amy Roberson, Rebecca Stuhr, and Leslie Gardner, have all provided resources and timely research assistance. At Grinnell, I have enjoyed being in a supportive cohort of faculty in my department and outside it. Steve Andrews, George Barlow, Elizabeth Dobbs, Mike Cavanagh, Heather Lobban-Viravong, Ralph Savarese, Erik Simpson, and Paula Smith made the department a supportive and collegial place. Vicki Bunnell, Lisa Mulholland, and Marna Montgomery in the English office have stepped in and saved the day many a time. The editorial staff of OSU Press kept this book on schedule. A special thanks is due to Sandy Crooms for her enthusiastic support.

For their friendship through some tumultuous years and for sustaining my life in Iowa with good humor, stimulating conversations, and some wonderful dinners, I thank Jenny Anger, Rachel Bly, Tim and Jen Dobe, Ed Gilday, Mike Guenther, Sue Ireland, Johanna Meehan, Elizabeth Prevost, Dan Reynolds, Garrett Roche, Alan and Jill Schrift, Sheila Schmidt, Tara Shukla, and Maura Strassberg. Anne Geissinger, amazing baker, excellent photographer, the kindest of friends, has shored up my life in more ways than I can count. Meena Khandelwal provided astute comments on my book proposal and she, Peter, Uma, and Jaya gave me a home away from home in Iowa City. It is only the least of my debts to Tyler Roberts that he read the entire manuscript and provided insightful comments; his love, friendship, and all the ways in which he shares in it, have enriched my life greatly.

Finally, there are long-standing debts to those who make my life in two continents possible. My brother Ashutosh has urged me to finish this book with his own brand of jokes and arguments, and on occasion has tracked down materials for me. He, Ishani, and Tanishi give me a second home in India. Usha Kapila, my mother, who has been a constant, nurturing presence in my life, reminds me that there are things other than work that make me who I am. My daughter Shivani (bringer of blessings) always shows me the way. This book was completed in the shadow of an enormous loss. My father, Ramesh Chandra Kapila—beloved parent who inspired my best work—passed away in August last year. I could not have imagined that he would not be present as I finished this book, and it is with great sadness and immense gratitude that I remember him for all the years of encouragement, faith, and love that enabled me to write it.

Chapter 2 is a version of Shuchi Kapila, "The Domestic Novel Goes Native: Bithia Mary Croker's Anglo-India" in *Nineteenth-Century Contexts* 26.3 (September 2004): 215–35, reprinted by permission of the publisher, Taylor & Francis Group (http://www.informaworld.com).

Thanks to Indiana University Press for permission to reprint a version of Shuchi Kapila, "Educating Seeta: Philip Meadows Taylor's Romances of Empire," *Victorian Studies* (Winter 1998) 41.2: 211–41 as chapter 4.

INTRODUCTION

The Poetics and Politics of Anglo-Indian Romance

I. Interracial Marriage and Colonial Domesticity

In late eighteenth-century India, Colonel Claude Martin (1735–1800) of the East India Company Army, who, like other Europeans in Lucknow, lived with many Indian wives or concubines, writes about his ward and later wife, Lise:

> My faithful girl called Boulone, or Lise, who has been most faithfully attached to me, and never had the smallest room to complain of her since I acquired her, which was when she was about nine years old, having brought her up, and educated her as my own child, with the most strictest, decent, and accomplished eastern education, having learned her to read and write Persian, and be strict in her religion, to which I found she was strictly adhered, as also to the purest virtue from a woman to her husband. Having always looked on her as such, and I have loved her as the most chaste virtuous wife. (qtd. in Archer 291)

As a romance narrative—regardless of the quality of his prose—this passage is striking for the smooth transition Martin makes from his relationship with a young girl of nine to his perception of her as his most loving wife. Lise was one of the many children that Claude Martin adopted whose Indian mothers remained in India while the fathers returned to Europe. She was purchased from his friend Carrière who had given her asylum when she fled from her father, Nawab Fazl Khan Bahadur, who had already killed her elder sister. She lived with Martin and grew so attached to him that when he offered to arrange a marriage for her a few years later, she insisted that she wanted to stay with him. She became his bibi[1] and later the mistress of his household.[2] Lise's history and Martin's comments about her encapsulate vividly the tropes in which colonial relationships between British men and Indian women were represented. Lise is educable, docile, devoted, and loyal, in other words, the ideal colonial subject. In a manner reminiscent of the sexual economy of the Victorian novel, she is both daughter and wife. She is rescued from her evil father by a benevolent Englishman. His roles as guardian, protector, husband, and colonizer share the same paternalism, making it easy for him to inhabit all these roles at once. Here, then, is a vignette of the perfect wife and subject around whom is built the romance of empire.

Educating Seeta makes the case that representations of such interracial relationships in the tropes of domestic fiction create a fantasy of liberal colonial rule in nineteenth-century British India. British colonials in India were preoccupied with appearing as a benevolent, civilizing power to their British and colonial subjects. They produced a vast archive of writing, which includes memoirs, official and private correspondence, and histories, in which they confronted their anxieties about their motives for colonial rule. I expand the definition of "family romance" to include not only interracial love between an English man and an Indian woman, but also political conflict represented as domestic drama featuring Indian women who appear in many roles: as widowed queens who act like recalcitrant daughters; as wives who bring domestic felicity but also usurp the English household; as heroic and rebellious natives; and as compliant and educable subjects. I argue that these seemingly disparate representations of Indian women all have the structure of a family romance,[3] a romance that portrays the permutations of interracial domesticity as a political allegory of indirect colonial rule. This Anglo-Indian[4] family romance—as I will call it here—thus becomes a particularly appropriate *literary* narrative that enables British writers to justify colonial rule as positive, educative, and benevolent. Two concepts, thus, become central to this study: first, that domestic fiction provides the tropes in which liberal British fantasies about India are represented, and second, that the presence of Indian women signals sites of crises in these fantasies.

The nature of British rule in India was a significant factor in shaping the form and structure of these literary-political fantasies. This was a system of "indirect rule" which was marked by policies that fostered rule by proxy rather than direct military takeover of Indian states, a concern with social and educational reform, and a consequent paternalism that stemmed from a belief in the superiority of British culture. Romances written in the context of this relationship between the British and Indians encode a political fantasy of creating through a process of benevolent rule, native subjects acculturated to European values who welcome colonial rule and ally themselves with British interests. The Englishman who is husband, teacher, father, and often benevolent administrator represents colonial patriarchy. The domestic Indian woman, whose docility represents political subservience, is the ideal native subject whose compliance can be won through a process of European education. However, this same woman becomes threatening when she assumes domestic or political power. *Educating Seeta* explores representations of colonial paternal authority in the Anglo-Indian romance and threats to this authority in the form of conflict in the family.

British portrayals of Indian women as compliant subjects do not remain uncontested even in their own writing: either the contradictions of colonialism defeat these narratives or the presence of Indian women who are active historical subjects forces colonial writers to confront the limits of their liberal desires. Thus Indian women in these romances point to another important aspect of the form: the fact that the hopes and desires of British administrators, writers, and travelers are not completely realized in these narratives. This failure to complete its allegory of successful colonial rule takes many narrative forms: ideological contradictions pointed out by Indian subjects; the inability of a British writer to carry through a narrative trajectory; and the power that Indian women assume in the home and outside that gives the lie to the "rescue" fantasy in which they are passive victims saved by Englishmen. Hence, given that the romance narrates the impossibility of neat conclusions, it seems more appropriate to describe it as a *failed* romance—one that does not reach its desired culmination. It is thus always marked by recognition of its failure even though it tries to seduce us into believing in the benevolence of colonial rule.

The death of the Indian woman in many of these romances, signaling that interracial love is not socially viable, is an instance of such narrative failure. For instance, in Flora Annie Steel's *On the Face of the Waters*, Zora dies early, setting the English hero, Jim Douglas, free to love an Englishwoman. There are, of course, exceptions to this rule, for instance in the Orientalist idealization of the Indian woman in Maud Diver's *Lilamani,* in which interracial marriage between Neville Sinclair and Lilamani heralds a new understanding between cultures with the ultimate goal of "civilizing" other cultures into European ways of life. Even Kipling, that canonized recorder of Anglo-Indian life, was unable to give us a full-length study of an interracial relationship. In most of his short stories, such relationships are unconsummated and end tragically.[5] Anglo-Indian romancers also seem reluctant to represent mixed-race children. When they do enter the picture, they are depicted with the same fear and horror that greeted miscegenation among white and black populations in nineteenth-century America. Despite these narrative failures, however, Anglo-Indian romancers do make a foray into imagining mixed households and interracial marriages. They execute a variety of formal explorations, which often surprise readers into confronting unorthodox outcomes about the possibilities of mixed race sociality.

A primary strategy of these romances is to chart British confrontation with a new, unfamiliar, and unprecedented cultural and political world and strive to make it familiar and coherent by domesticating protest, opposition, and hybridity. They thus stay anchored in the colony, and even those that end tragically force the reader to recognize the consequences of a culturally mixed space. They refigure adventure and domestic fiction by engaging with racial difference, interracial desire, and miscegenation. In this respect they can be distinguished from the conventions of Victorian fiction in which race, gender, and geography are all neatly aligned to provide domestic closure, which is based on the exclusion and elimination of such differences. *Educating Seeta* thus argues that interracial romances in British India are more than simple love-stories; they express and contest class, gender, and racial ideologies formed during the colonial encounter.

This versatility of the Anglo-Indian romance in incorporating both colonial desires and their disruptions can be attributed to its foundation in representations of domestic life which has a wider range of reference to the social-political world than the language of romance usually suggests.[6] In invoking "the domestic," I refer to a complex web of ideas and historically specific meanings usually associated with the middle class. Domesticity is embedded in a matrix of other discourses—social, political, legal, and sexual—that are particularly significant in a study of the romance plot of heterosexual marriage.[7] We now have a rich and substantial scholarship that shows that the relation of the domestic sphere to the outside world of business and politics, and to definitions of gender and self, has been in flux throughout the nineteenth century.[8] However, the conceptual centrality accorded to domestic ideology in the Victorian era has only recently been transferred to the English household in the colonies. When Victorian domesticity is recreated in the colonies, the British home comes to signify culture, nation, class, and race. The domestic functions of surveillance and management come to acquire a particular urgency in the colonies and appear, in effect, to be an extension of imperial governance. Commenting on the advice given to English housewives by Maud Diver in *The Englishwoman in India* (1909), Rosemary George points to the language of "state-craft and diplomacy" in which housewives are urged to aspire to the role of "the politically astute leader who holds the reins of empire in his hands" (George 51). Similarly Steel and Gardiner in their *The Complete Indian Housekeeper and Cook* (1890) write, "We do not wish to cultivate an unholy haughtiness; but an Indian household can no more be governed peacefully, without dignity and prestige, than an Indian Empire" (qtd. in George 51). George comments, "Time and again, the colonial discourse, especially the texts written by women, represent the management of empire as essentially 'home-management' on a large scale. There are doors to be locked, corners to be periodically dusted, rooms to be fumigated and made free of pests, children (i.e.,"natives") to be doctored, educated, clothed, disciplined, accounts to be kept, boundaries redrawn and fences mended" (George 51). The English home thus reinforces the allegorical structure of the relationship between domestic life and politics in both of which natives are in a position of tutelage to British men and women.

The other side of the English household in the colonies was the Indian domestic space, which, to British eyes, appeared to be a baffling network of intrigue, mobility, and diffuse power. In a groundbreaking study of slavery and kinship in an upper-class eighteenth-century Bengal household, Indrani Chatterjee shows how indirect rule, domestic life, ownership of land, and ideas about gender were all interconnected and that these ideas were being worked out in the confused mess created by the struggle between fluid ideas of kin in Indian households and the more rigid notions of family in English law. The division of the household into the women's quarters or 'harem' and the outer public space did not map onto English notions of private and public because though Indian women were secluded, matriarchs often wielded considerable political power by controlling access to young women of reproductive age and hence lineage and inheritance.[9] Matriarchs also gave advice to ruling princes or regent, negotiated political alliances, and used their diplomatic skills and wealth for political ends.[10] This politically active function of women was routinely looked upon with suspicion by British colonial administrators. The customary ability of mothers to adopt successors and create lineages by marrying off their wards came into direct confrontation with the economic and territorial designs of the East India Company.

In response to these confusing networks of kinship and sociality, colonial ideology tried to impose a rigorously policed notion of the domestic in Anglo-Indian culture as a way of consolidating class and racial status. Anglo-Indian romances, however, register the struggle over domestic space which unsettles Victorian notions of gender, culture, and class. They combine realist conventions of representing domesticity with fantasy, history, and the forbidden subject of interracial mixing. Rejecting the language of sexual pathology, "encounter," or a feminized Orient, they thus offer an alternative focus on colonial experience by mixing historical, political, and legislative dilemmas into their domestic dramas. Unlike adventure fiction, these romances record the disruptive presence of Indian wives and rebellious subjects who resist being cast as passive female bodies ruled by masculine colonizers. Instead, these romances show that interracial domesticity encodes differing modalities of power for both British colonial and Indian subjects, a joint negotiation of social and political position, and an engagement with the possibility of a mixed cultural life.

Interracial domesticity thus provides us a way to understand the processes of collaboration, assimilation, and a seemingly nonviolent negotiation of cultural intermixing between the two populations. As Ann Stoler has convincingly shown us in her work on the Netherlands Indies, colonial social life was central to the construction of bourgeois ideology. She argues that domestic ideologies, which were central to bourgeois life, were about much more than just sex. They encompassed a wider range of desires and yearnings, which were encoded within a larger range of colonial relations than the repressive model of sexuality would suggest. The importance of racial intermixing was that "the changing density and intensity of métissage's discursive field outlines the fault lines of colonial authority: in linking domestic arrangements to the public order, family to the state, sex to subversion, and psychological essence to racial type, métissage might be read as a metonym for the biopolitics of empire at large" (Stoler, "Tensions" 199).[11] Similarly Durba Ghosh has argued in her study of the family and sex in colonial India, that "interracial sexual relationships were a crucial and constitutive part of early colonial state formation and governance in British India, laying the foundation for the colonial social order" (Ghosh "Sex and The Family" 2). She emphasizes the importance of studying the family unit in colonial culture because it echoes patriarchal authority in other colonial institutions such as the courts, the military, and the church (Ghosh "Sex and the Family" 4).

Until the recent wave of colonial cultural studies, most historians ignored interracial romances between European colonizers and native women as a marginal and colorful byproduct of colonialism that did not teach us much about colonial society. One reason for this neglect could be that interracial love, and its corollary, the possibility of miscegenation, while it has always existed in colonial societies, has also been proscribed in official ideologies of most such societies. In the case of colonial India particularly, the absence of discussion about interracial relationships could be because such relationships were visible largely in the last two decades of the eighteenth century.[12]

Given official disapproval of such relationships in India, it is not surprising that the women involved were rendered invisible in the colonial archive. It was feminist scholars who used the tools of interdisciplinary inquiry to prise open the archive in order to catch a glimpse of women's lives during colonialism and to argue that the politics of gender are constitutive of colonial culture. For instance, even though Indian women appear frequently in late-eighteenth- and nineteenth-century British writings as faithful wives, rebellious queens, and ideal colonial subjects, their fragmentary presence made them inconsequential to most colonial literary studies.[13] Feminist projects of recovering the voices of these women have produced some of the most exciting and productive studies of South Asian colonial culture. Whether it was Gayatri Spivak's reading of the silence of the queen-as-figurehead in her essay "The Rani of Sirmur" or Lata Mani's (1959) work on the Sati (self-immolating widow), such studies have offered new methods and theories of reading silences and absences in the colonial archive.

If historical accounts have been slow to recognize the significance of interracial desire, literature, on the other hand, seems obsessed with it. In inverse relation to the decline in interracial relationships, literary writing about them increased substantially through the late nineteenth century. Robert Young reminds us that miscegenation and hybridity are the foundational narratives of most Victorian and modern fiction. "English experience," he writes, "is characterized by a sense of fluidity and a painful sense of, or need for, otherness" (Young 2). This crossing over into otherness is often accomplished through the medium of interracial desire in "the Brontës, Hardy or Lawrence . . . (the irresistible, transgressive Heathcliff is of mixed race), Haggard, Conrad (not only *The Secret Agent*, but also of course in *Heart of Darkness*, the imbrication of the two cultures within each other, the fascination with the 'magnificent' African woman, and among many other novels, his first, *Almayer's Folly*, the story of an inter-racial marriage), James, Forster, Cary, Lawrence, Joyce, Greene, Rhys" (Young 2–3). As a counterpoint to Young's view that the English novel compulsively invokes the other in erotic, sexual terms, I argue, however, that the ultimate rejection of the alien Other is equally a distinctive strategy of the English domestic novel. While desire for the Other has frequently been depicted in high Victorian and modern fiction, it is invariably portrayed as futile, unconsummated, and tragic. Canonical English fiction describes interracial romance as reified and dream-like, merely a projection of English anxieties rather than transformative of English fictional conventions. Young recognizes the subterranean nature of such desire when he calls it "the soft underbelly of that power relation" that was colonial rule (Young 175). As long as English writers describe such desire in the language of repression and projection, they deny, repress, and eventually expel it.[14]

In fact, Victorian novelists have generally distanced themselves from a concern with colonialism, international trade and commerce, and the consequences at home of cultural exchange abroad. Gayatri Spivak and Edward Said, in their much-celebrated interventions, brought the insights of colonial and postcolonial studies to bear on a reading of the seemingly insular domestic novel.[15] Their insight that colony and metropole, the international division of labor, and the histories of colonialism and oppression are constitutive of the aesthetic conventions of the novel, have been brilliantly followed through in studies of nineteenth-century fiction.[16]

However, while recognizing the mutual imbrication of colony and nation has been a necessary move in colonial studies, it is equally important to study the gestures of repudiation and banishment of the colonial by the domestic English world. Even if astute critics mine the domestic for its connections with the colonial through metaphor, in the end the colonies are occluded for a return to English civility in the home. As Clara Tuite points out, in Jane Austen's *Mansfield Park*, for instance, "colonial critique is subordinated to and chastised by the impulses of domestic drama," and ultimately, "the world of the colonies is represented or subsumed by the terms of representation of the other world of the domestic" (Tuite 104). This subordination of the colonial to the domestic English suggests to me that the canonical nineteenth-century novel does not allow us to explore the possibilities of interracial romance, banishing it either to the margins of the text or refusing it admission into the narrative altogether. This is where the Anglo-Indian romance comes in as a necessary supplement to the Victorian novel. In all its manifestations in literary texts, histories, and other colonial writing, it enables an exploration of interracial romance, and through that, colonial sociality.

The contributions of the Anglo-Indian romance to our understanding of Victorian culture are evident in recent studies that show how events in England and India refracted, impacted, and transformed perceptions of Victorian England and the colonies simultaneously, and that the domestic and political were intimately related. Gayatri Spivak, Jenny Sharpe, Dierdre David, Nancy Paxton, Sara Suleri, John McBratney, Parama Roy, Siraj Ahmed, and others have focused specifically on the fact that Britain's Indian experience had profound ideological and formal consequences for English literature.[17] For instance, the divorce debates in England were seen as a kind of revolt, while the Indian Revolt of 1857 was imagined as a marriage gone wrong.[18] A similar conceptual and linguistic osmosis characterized discussions about the Rani of Jhansi who was read as counterpoint or double of Queen Victoria. The fear of an unruly woman on the throne is projected onto the Rani of Jhansi articulating a similar latent British fear about Queen Victoria (Jerinic 127). British writers considered good government masculine and entirely separate from domestic influence, but issues related to sexuality and domesticity spilled into the public world of government. Debates related to adoption, property, and customary rights did not stay confined to the private sphere but assumed a political significance.

Educating Seeta combines literary methodologies for reading textual silences with a new Historicist understanding that cultural concepts circulate in different guises through all contemporary texts. The texts chosen for analysis were all written by British subjects in India, and this specific site of the production of colonial ideology is as significant as the fact that these are "English" texts that try to produce English cultural forms and values. The focus on textual production follows the example of colonial discourse analysis, but with a difference. While studies of the rhetoric of Britain's colonial experience in India have emphasized the role of native and colonial elites in jointly forging colonial culture, and have explored the aesthetics and politics of collaboration, complicity, and shared guilt, I stay committed to the notion that a colonial will drove and attempted to structure the agendas of imperial control, and that these were neither incidental nor accidental.

A focus on the "detail of cultural facticity"(Suleri 13) can reveal not only complicity but also show how the larger narratives of empire were locally and variously contested, overwhelmed, modified, seized, and redeployed, or superseded. Thus, while remaining sensitive to class compacts and the role of elites, I am equally interested in uncovering resistance to colonial agendas, whether they involve the efficient functioning of colonial government or the organization of a home. I argue, therefore, for the special function of literary texts in articulating these agendas and revealing their limits and conclude that literary narratives were alibis for the "benevolence" and "high civility" of empire. However, equally important to this study are those documents and writings (letters, memoirs, histories) that place literature in the larger context of colonial experience and hence bring the particularity of literary agendas to light.

In *Educating Seeta,* I emphasize contradictions embedded in the project of "civilizing" Indians which, methodologically, is also the place from which to recover those native voices that inhabit the interstitial spaces in the colonial archive. I resist, therefore, a view of colonial power and surveillance that is seamless and all-encompassing. This emphasis is what distinguishes my argument from, for instance, Anindyo Roy's discussion of the same historical moment in his *Civility and Empire* in which he links civility to civic virtue and civil identity. Roy sees civility as representing a particular ethos that secured "those powerful ideologies of modern citizenship that came to be linked to Britain's status as an emerging imperial power" (Roy 10). Roy's argument lays out in great detail both the social spaces that are controlled by colonial rulers and the fact that disciplinary regimes manifest themselves by "defining and monitoring the social behavior of colonial subjects" (Roy 12). But even though he gestures towards the contradictions that mark the terrain on which colonial rule establishes itself, these contradictions do not assume a large or threatening presence in the relentless march of colonialism. Against this perspective, I present the inherently fractured and incomplete project of British colonial rule, and the insertion of unruly colonized natives into this terrain as presenting insurmountable problems. I read the fracture of colonial civility as productive moments of protest against colonial power and as places where British colonials recognize the impossibility of their projects. When I analyze a "successful" interracial marriage, it is to note the messiness of cultural exchange rather than the disciplining of native bodies by English discourses. A study of colonial culture through the romance makes possible a dual focus on the aspirations and failures of British colonial rule.

II. Indian Women in Colonial Texts

The recurrence of the Indian woman in colonial writing and her interpellation as the ideal native subject has two distinct but related sources in colonial history. The first is the fact that the woman question was central to Orientalist,[19] Utilitarian, and Evangelical writings on Indian history.[20] In Utilitarian accounts of Indian history, the best known being James Mill's *History of India,* Hindu society is described as in a state of degeneration, an index of which is the condition of its women, who then require British protection and intervention. In Orientalist constructions of a "golden age" of Vedic civilization, most prominently in the work of Orientalist scholars such as Henry Colebrook (1765–1837) and William Jones (1746–94), founder of the Asiatic Society of Bengal, the Hindu woman had a privileged place. Conflating Hindu with Indian culture, they believed that ancient Hindu society had been advanced because it allowed its women considerable social freedom. Following eighteenth-century notions that the index of a civilized culture was the freedom it allowed its women, Orientalist scholars concluded that the low status of women in contemporary Hindu society was a visible sign of its fallen state. This belief supported the idea that natives who were originally noble and civilized had to be educated as citizens of a modern state. In idealizing the status of women in ancient India, the Orientalists ignored internal social hierarchies which oppressed women of lower classes and castes; nevertheless, their work drew the attention of reformers and administrators to an ideal drawn from Hindu culture for the respect and social status accorded to Hindu women.

The second historical reason for the prominence of the Hindu woman in the colonial imagination can be traced to the famous legislation of 1829 against the practice of Sati (widow immolation), which provided protection to widows of upper-caste Hindus from the practice of forced immolation on the funeral pyres of their husbands. This legislation was preceded by furious debates in England and India which recreated vivid images of helpless women oppressed by heathen obscurantism.[21] The fascination with Sati also meant that the upper-caste Hindu woman came to stand in for all Hindu women, in complete disregard of the contestations within customary practice and the fact that there was a lower incidence of Sati among women of lower castes.[22] The Sati controversy thus easily leant itself to a rescue fantasy in which the Indian woman at the mercy of abominable heathen customs is rescued by the benevolent Englishman. Margery Sabin describes this narrative of the saving of a Sati by British officers as "an old pattern of romance: the Hindu widow is the touching female victim of enchantment; the British rescuer has the heart, if not always the power, of a chivalric hero.... More honour than burden the mission of civilization in the early nineteenth century offered a modern arena for noble deeds" (Sabin, "Suttee Romance" 3–4). Colonial administrators and politicians, the main actors in this drama, perceived the heroic potential in the acting out of their political and administrative missions in rescuing the Indian woman from oppressive social customs.

I argue here that this scenario changes by the mid-nineteenth century when the romance evolves into a distinct form to articulate the concerns of a changing colonial ideology moving away from the idea of "rescue." With the development of indirect rule, India was no longer a mythical world but an administrative challenge; a land not of fabled riches but of economic hardship; a scene not for noble deeds but for mercantile gains and strategic political games. At this historical conjuncture "the failed family romance" became particularly appropriate as a representation of colonizer/colonized relations, as a fable about cultural assimilation, and as a fantasy about ideal political subjects. *Educating Seeta* intervenes in this discussion with the argument that it was not only the Sati that became familiar to British audiences. Images of high-caste, aristocratic widows deprived of their estates or prevented from adopting a son haunted the liberal British imagination as evidence of the depredations of colonial rule and thus a taint on British honor and virtue. This connection was most famously established in Edmund Burke's impassioned Parliamentary address in 1788 seeking the impeachment of Warren Hastings.[23] In his attack on Hastings, Burke described the evils of colonialism in images of sexualized assault on high-born women, particularly the Begums of Oudh.[24] Burke's exposé of the fate of such women is only part of the story, however. The other version has its greatest exemplar in the life of the widowed Rani of Jhansi. She asserted her right to adopt an heir and refused to cede her kingdom to the East India Company. She was fatally wounded in the ensuing battle against British forces and commemorated as a hero and rebel by Indians. The Mutiny of 1857, prompted in part by popular sympathy for the Rani, turned this encounter into legend. Other Indian women rulers waged equally persistent if less visibly heroic battles against British authority. In literary fantasies, Indian women in political or domestic roles either present a direct political threat to English power or to the English household and ultimately to imperial power.[25]

The challenges of working with the fragmentary appearance of the Indian woman in the archive have produced crucial methodological and theoretical insights for historical and literary studies of the colonial period. In *Reading the East India Company Archive,* Betty Joseph exhorts postcolonial critics to "show why the domain of women's agency has been excluded from mainstream accounts and demonstrate, at the same time, how women are put together as subjects and objects of various discourses for the ruses and deployments of colonial power" (Joseph 4). As a corrective to the common notion that women are excluded from the colonial archive, Joseph points out that they are, in fact, found everywhere, though "in a fragmented and dispersed way" (Joseph 93). As Joseph explains, such appearances of the figure of the woman not only provide "historical articulations of the discursive networks and their relationship to each other, but also makes woman, in her role as constitutive exclusion, a deconstructive lever for revealing how various sites and arenas of history are repressed at various moments" (Joseph 4). Following a similar strategy, *Educating Seeta* uncovers the inscription of women both as an alternative history of colonial social relations, and as a trace of their acts of assertion and protest.

This discussion of the silencing of the Indian woman was pioneered by Spivak in "The Rani of Sirmur" in which a widowed Indian queen of an annexed state in nineteenth-century India is "suddenly managed by a young white man in her own household" (267). Declaring that "there is no romance to be found here," Spivak exposes the expedient use of religious ideologies for political purposes by both colonial and native patriarchy when the Rani's fate is determined by a British representative in conjunction with native scholars (should she commit Sati on her husband's funeral pyre or should she continue as figurehead of the state?) (Spivak, "Sirmur" 267). Spivak's reading of the colonial moment in which the Rani is discovered maps out not only the complex interrelations between colonial authority and a patriarchal regulation of the lives of the native aristocracy but also the instrumentality of the queen, who appears in the record only when she is required to facilitate colonial rule.

In presenting a cast of women characters from colonial history who are neither completely silent nor objects of rescue, I interrogate Gayatri Spivak's comment about the absence of romance derived from a similar moment in colonial history. I would argue that in making her point, she generalizes from a colonial record that provides numerous counterinstances of women of ruling families caught in legal, political, and administrative confrontations with the East India Company, who actively protested against the imposition of British law on their lives. Instead of a record of silences, I uncover a proliferation of romance narratives, those of the East India Company as *paterfamilias* and the women rulers as their obedient daughters. The misogynist images of incompetent queens or queen mothers, ill-advised regents, and helpless widows who are trained into compliance by the Company are the obverse of the romance in which the upper-class Indian woman is saved and educated by a sympathetic Englishman. So while my approach to the representation of Indian women draws on the insights of feminist literary critics and historians, particularly the idea that the fragmentary appearance and extreme marginality of Indian women marks the fissures and faultlines of colonial legislation, administrative organization, and gender and domestic ideologies, I turn to a different kind of material from that which forms the basis of the studies mentioned above. In the literary romances, letters, memoirs, and political correspondence discussed here, Indian women appear as major actors. Whether it is fiction, political correspondence, or personal letters, each of these appearances express British colonial anxiety about the limitations and contradictions of liberal colonialism.

Highlighting the participation of women in colonial history is an ongoing critical endeavor, judging by the predominance and visibility of men in such histories. Françoise Vèrges, for instance, bases her study of colonial family romance in the French colony of Réunion Island on Lynn Hunt's concept of the French family romance.[26] Vèrges defines "family romance" as "a fiction created by the *colonial power* that substituted a set of imaginary parents, La Mère-Patrie and her children the colonized, for the real parents of the colonized, who were slaves, colonists, and indentured workers . . . " (Vèrges 3–4; emphasis in original). La Mère-Patrie, a single entity, replaces the two parents of the colonized and brings the promise of rule among equals against the local tyrants. In her study of the anticolonial debates around métissage, most of which emphasized assimilation and full admission into the promise of the French Republic for the freed brothers of Réunion Island, Vèrges concludes that the liberal promise of equal French citizenship fails when racial and cultural difference prevents the métis population from attaining that goal. Significantly, in a study devoted to colonial politics cast as family drama, Vèrges deals exclusively with "the band of brothers." As she acknowledges in the epilogue to her book, "the history of Réunion's women remains to be told, and this study has not given them their due" (Vèrges 249).

Like Vèrges, I explore interracial romance as a fiction created by the colonizers, as a promise of a benevolent regime which produces happy assimilated and loyal families. Like Vèrges, I also argue that the colonial patriarch in British Indian writing establishes kinship with the natives through tutelage and patronage. The East India Company in colonial India becomes "Ma-Baap" or "Mother-Father," a single entity which represents political and familial authority. The romance thus becomes an allegory of colonial relations in which racial and cultural difference is absorbed and domesticated. *Educating Seeta* traces a similar narrative of failure when the promise of a happy conclusion to an interracial marriage or complete citizenship for an Indian subject under liberal British rule is thwarted time and again. The significant difference is that the focus of *Educating Seeta* is on *colonized* women who appear as obedient daughters and wives in heterosexual, domestic narratives. *Educating Seeta* concerns itself not only with a literary narrative produced by British colonials to justify the benevolence and success of colonial rule, but also with Indian women as actors. I point out how this narrative, once available, was deployed rhetorically and politically by colonized women to resist being incorporated into British colonial narratives. In my chapters on the widowed queens of Indian states, for instance, I show how the language of familial civility is used by them to demand their rights as subjects of the East India Company, and when that fails, to reject the romance of liberal rule altogether. The idea of romance thus is mobile and multivalent. It disrupts any conception of linear and absolute power, showing instead the space of struggle and negotiation both among British colonials and their Indian subjects.

Indian women become actors in these texts not because they are reflecting a state of historical empowerment. They are present precisely because I am arguing that both in history and in literary texts an excess of signification, of meaning, attaches to the figure of the Indian woman. I have tried to move back and forth between her historical presence and her appearance as a literary figure. By doing this, I hope to trace the trajectory of colonial desire, and also its disruptions when the figure of the Indian woman appears. Instead of being defeated by the fragmentary, seemingly incoherent inscription of the Indian woman, an exploration of interracial romance brings to light not only these women but also colonial ideologies and alternative historical narratives.

III. *The Poetics and Politics of Romance*

I identify four romance narratives in colonial writing; some overlap with others, but all involve the home and interracial domesticity. The first and most common is the "rescue" story.[27] Company officials who adopt young native girls, either to provide them refuge against oppressive cultural injunctions or from political persecution, marry these girls when they reach adolescence. The introduction begins with an example of such a relationship between Claude Martin and Lise. This narrative of rescue attaches to most interracial romances, even those that ultimately become more complex records of domestic partnership between an English man and Indian woman. In many cases, the adolescent Indian girl is not a ward of the Englishman, but is rescued at an extremely young age from her natal family and incorporated into a covert interracial romance. Among the most famous of such partnerships are those between James Achilles Kirkpatrick and Khair-un-nissa and William Gardner and the daughter of the Nawab of Cambay. The power of this colonial narrative is evident in the fact that even though in both cases the rescue narrative encapsulates very little of the subsequent life of these couples, both men feel compelled to narrate their connection to these women as originating in a benevolent act of rescue. The persistence and reach of rescue narratives has made it seem that they were the only kind available in which British colonials could present their encounter with India. Jyotsna Singh points out that "the tropes of discovery, civilization, and rescue . . . have survived beyond the classic colonial era and continue to color our perceptions of the non-Western world" (Singh 5). Gayatri Spivak famously noted that white men rescuing brown women from brown men was the foundational fantasy on which civil society was based in colonial India.[28] *Educating Seeta* goes beyond this obvious narrative to show the further development of colonial stories of rescue into domestic tales; it also explores the political desires that underpin these fantasies.

A second kind of nineteenth-century interracial romance is usually in the high Orientalist mode and does not dwell on either the contribution of the Indian companions to the creation of a syncretic upper-class culture, the role of such alliances in the acquisition and management of political power, or the process by which they were justified in private and political circles. Such exercises in Orientalist fiction include Sydney Owenson's *The Missionary: an Indian Tale* (1811), Maud Diver's *Lilamani* (1911), and Philip Meadows Taylor's *Seeta* (1872). The women in these novels, melancholy, "idealized," exotic beauties who represent not only the glories of Hindu culture but also its repressive aspects, are rescued by Englishmen. The attempt to match two glorious civilizations flounders when the inevitable racial differences are confronted. Maud Diver's trilogy, of which *Lilamani* is the first part, is unusual in taking the story through many generations. Most such interracial stories come to an unhappy end before their authors confront the question of mixed children.

In the third form of interracial romance, British writers represent interracial relationships through a "scandal," which makes the private life of a British man the subject of an official and public discussion. In such cases, different versions of the romance collide, overlap, and are in turn contradicted in the private correspondence of the men. The self-representations of British men, their defense of themselves, and their search for an appropriate narrative in which to record their lives, shows the contradictions of this version of the family romance when confronted with official British ideology.

Educating Seeta offers a fourth version of the romance, which focuses on the specific conditions of indirect rule in which British representatives supervise the organization of the households and estates of widowed queens of Indian states. Though they are not domestic partners in the usual sense, the queens and British representatives create the kinds of domestic dramas that constitute the Anglo-Indian family romance. In histories of the annexation of Indian states, conflict about household expenses becomes central to the relationship between women heads of state and British Residents. The resulting negotiations about domestic life make political relations of dependency and subservience rather than blood relationships significant.

The book is divided into two parts consisting of two chapters, each of which begins with a historical introduction to the context of interracial romances. The first part includes two chapters: the first studies the epistolary record of an interracial romance between an Englishman, William Linneaus Gardner, and his aristocratic Muslim wife, Mah Munzalool nissa Begum; the second chapter focuses on Bithia Mary Croker's early twentieth-century romances, which represent interracial relationships at a time when official proscriptions against them were really strong. Both chapters explore British representations of mixed domesticity; the construction of class, racial, and national identity in the mixed household; and the place of the Indian woman in this literary-political domain. By focusing on the mixed household as either a place of intense social negotiation or of a gothic, traumatic discovery, I show that interracial domesticity is a nodal point for the cultural and political negotiations of Britain's Indian experience. Mixed households contest the values of English domesticity and reconfigure interracial relationships away from the predictable tropes of rescue and discovery to an exploration of how class and social power were acquired by colonial elites.

The second part discusses inscriptions of indirect rule in fictional and nonfictional writing in nineteenth-century India. Here again, my dual emphasis is on exploring the nature of British colonial fantasies and their failures when contested by Indian women. Chapter 3 discusses the annexations of the central Indian states of Satara, Sambhalpur, Nagpur, and Jhansi, foregrounding the role played by the queens in political negotiations with the British. I analyze the preoccupations of historians of this period in which, though Indian women are pervasive, they are often silenced. The trope of a benevolent colonial state in search of good daughters appears in historical writings of the period as well as its literary texts. Chapter 4 takes another episode from this history, this time located in a south Indian state, and shows the relationship between Philip Meadows Taylor's political dealings with the Queen of Shorapur and his literary writings. Such a study is less concerned with causality or simplistic translation of the historical record into a literary fantasy; rather it seeks common tropes and narratives in which the British colonial experience in India was being imagined and recorded and identifies the manner in which literary texts sought to transform the messiness of historical, political struggle into idealized and sentimental narratives.

By juxtaposing a literary and historical chapter in each of the two sections in *Educating Seeta*, I am suggesting that they draw on similar narratives, techniques of emplotment, and cultural fantasies. This relationship between literature and history has been theorized at length by Hayden White, who argues that both literature and history depend on specific devices of emplotment and figures of speech to weave their narratives. The primary material of history is unstructured and chaotic, and historians, as much as writers of creative fiction, shape their work into culturally recognizable narratives. White's theories were a response to the bourgeois realistic conventions of historical writing which, he argued, incorrectly assumed the priority of 'facts' and convinced readers of these facts through the aesthetic conventions of realism. His arguments, which pushed for an understanding of historical writing through the laws of representation, have continued to produce questions about the status of 'reality' or referentiality in such writing.[29]

White's theories have been criticized by both literary critics and historians for establishing an absolute parity between literary and historical narratives. In responding to his critics, especially in the debate about revisionist histories of the Holocaust, White has moved towards giving historical writing its own priorities which delimit and circumscribe its concerns in a manner different from those found in literary narratives. Particularly useful for my argument is the view derived from White's later work that referential considerations are important in historical texts because they affect the system of signification and the codes of representation in such texts. One consequence of this is that "historical narrative thus seems unable to fully utilize the full effect of the fictionalization that it purportedly performs" (Pihlainen 54).[30] The fact that histories follow events documented in many different genres of writing, and that they deal with events that happened to particular people, keep them committed to a certain set of conventions which might not follow the rules of literary emplotment. So even though the literary and the historical seem to be one continuous narrative, I argue that while literary texts idealize their characters, narrative outcome, and plot, historical texts seem committed to documenting a variety of colonial experiences without forcing it into the formal or predetermined closures of literary narratives. For instance, the literary idea of the Indian damsel-in-distress rescued by the dashing English knight turns out to be inadequate for capturing all the features of Gardner's domestic life. His historical record of the social, political, and material details of his mixed household grow and overwhelm the rescue story with which his relationship with his wife began.

In their propensity to dwell in realms of fantasy and speculation, romances suggest utopian resolutions of insurmountable class, caste, familial, or religious antagonisms. I borrow this concept of romance as an allegory of political struggle from Doris Sommer's study of nineteenth-century Latin American fiction, in which she shows how "erotic and romantic rhetoric organizes apparently nonviolent national consolidation during periods of internecine conflict" in Latin American history (Sommer, "Irresistible Romance" 76). In Sommer's foundational fictions, desire for an ideal nation is not merely parallel to romantic desire, it creates the conditions in which romantic desire can flourish so that one constitutes the other. It thus has a performative function, acting to seduce and persuade the reader that romantic reconciliation is a model for political alliances in the future. Anglo-Indian romances are similarly marked by a desire for harmonious reconciliation and new alliances. Early in my discussion, I introduced the idea of 'failure' of the Anglo-Indian romance. Following Doris Sommer's complex and very relevant argument about how allegory operates in the world of the nineteenth-century Latin American "national" novels, it would be possible to connect this failure to the structure of allegory itself. Sommer is interested, however, in celebrating the "incredible measure of their success" ("Allegory" 81) as erotic-political allegories rather than their failures. Further, by coining the word "dialectical-allegories" to describe the "collusion between passion and patriotism" ("Allegory" 80), Sommer points to a lack in the critical vocabulary in which we discuss the novel and the romance today. In showing us the limits of our current understanding of allegory, Sommer forges a new connection between desire, politics, and narrative that she considers as relevant to our modern appreciation and enjoyment of literature as it was in its nineteenth-century Latin American context.

Sommer's infusion of a dialectical view of history into allegory is highly suggestive for my analysis of the Anglo-Indian romance. I am going to argue, however, that both British colonial history in India and the presence of Indian subjects in the texts analyzed in *Educating Seeta* make the *failure* of the allegory a more significant theoretical category than the successes that Sommer celebrates in the Latin American context. This discussion of failure and allegory requires a brief review of Sommer's argument and Walter Benjamin's writings on allegory. Taking up Paul de Man's reading of Rousseau's *Julie*, Sommer argues against his point that those who pass "'from individual passions such as love, to the collective and social dimensions of the state' are, or should be, . . . embarrassed" (Sommer, "Allegory" 69). For Sommer, the supersession of love and politics by a nondialectical religious experience does not work. It assumes a dimension of stable knowledge that she resists. In contrast to this, Benjamin matches allegory and dialectics and attempts to "salvage allegory for historical narrative" (Sommer 63). Instead of a transcendent and immanent level of reality, Sommer's definition of reality is more interested in Benjamin's categories of nature and history. Benjamin argues that allegory is not merely a double narrative in which the mundane stands transparently for another transcendental reality. Rather, it incorporates within it a dialectical relationship between two levels of signification. As Sommer points out, Benjamin associated allegory with a melancholic sense of the distance between sign and referent, and hence with an inescapable recognition of failure. In his essay "Allegory and Trauerspiel" in *The Origin of German Tragedy*, he writes:

> Whereas in the symbol destruction is idealized and the transfigured face of nature is fleetingly revealed in the light of redemption, in allegory the observer is confronted with the *facies hippocratica* of history as a petrified, primordial landscape. Everything about history that, from the very beginning, has been untimely, sorrowful, unsuccessful, is expressed in a face—or rather in a death's head. (Benjamin 168)

The philosophic association between history, decay, and human nature that Benjamin considers central to the allegory provides a conceptual template for our understanding of the incommensurability of interracial romance and liberal politics, their failure to mesh together seamlessly that is encoded in the Anglo-Indian romance. Instead of a tale that ends happily ever after, bringing together the domestic and the political, this allegory marks the impossibility of such a culmination. In confronting the difference between history and its idealized representation, as between sign and referent, the Anglo-Indian romance is allegorical in precisely the way that Benjamin describes it.

Temporal distance between the referents and the illusion of completeness both lead to the failure of perfect correspondence between the two parts of an allegory. The illusion of complete correspondence is recognized as an illusion and temporal distance serves to emphasize the spaces between narratives rather than show their perfect cohesion. As Stephen Melville writes, "Allegory has a way of insisting on this problematic—on the uncertainty, at every moment, of the relation between a given present or claim to presence and the narratives—stories and histories—by which it is traversed and in which it should figure" (Melville 81). Even if allegory were the perfect literary figure for the texts I analyze, interracial romance narratives always show the impossibility and uncertainty of claims to British benevolence. In the case of British colonial narratives, allegory is meant to suggest the larger political narrative of benevolent colonialism. In doing that it is actually writing that other narrative, seducing us into believing it exists. In that sense, its role is performative in the way Sommer suggests. However, once you consider them 'fictional compensations,' they inscribe their own failure because they stand in for events, conciliations, conclusions that don't really happen. Certainly, Benjamin's idea of dialectics would explain how the centrality of Indian women to legislative and social reform made them ideal citizens, both stories mutually constructing each other, contiguous and coexstensive. However, historical events in colonial India fail to achieve the perfection of allegorical form precisely because they are in excess of that literary structure. Allegory, in this case, marks the difference between history and its idealized representation.

Part I

Of Bibis and Begums
Company Affairs in Colonial India

Interracial relationships in late-eighteenth century India rarely excited adverse comment, becoming visible only if there was a "scandal" attached to them or when the wills of British men became public. This was especially true of upper-class relationships because such scandals were read as a betrayal of national and racial identity.[1] Other kinds of liaisons between Indian women and soldiers, writers, and other employees of the East India Company did not raise so much dust because they could be dealt with as just an administrative problem. However, whenever British men in positions of power were called upon to justify or defend their unorthodox choice of domestic partners, they wrote elaborate defenses of their English identity. These fascinating texts reproduce the racial and cultural values of imperialism even as they try to reconcile their "English" values with their obvious breach of them.

The high incidence of interracial liaisons between men of the elite classes in the Company and upper-class Muslim women in the Presidencies can be explained by the affluence of East India Company officials which, when combined with the consolidation of the Company's power in late-eighteenth-century India, inspired imitation of the Indian aristocracy. Diplomatic maneuvering with native aristocrats also facilitated personal relationships between British officials and Indian upper classes, which expressed both a class compact and an intermixing of cultures that was not repeated in the same way at any other point in Indo-British history.

A list of notable men who maintained interracial households with Indian women shows the astonishing prevalence of this lifestyle: Charles Warre Malet, governor of Bombay; John Wombwell, East Indian Company paymaster at Lucknow; Claude Martin, adventurer, courtier, amateur scientist in Lucknow; Colonel Antoine-Louis-Henri Polier (a Swiss Protestant of French descent) who served in the army of the British East India Company; James Achilles Kirkpatrick, Resident at Hyderabad; William Palmer, Secretary to Warren Hastings; and William Linneaus Gardner, founder of Gardner's Horse. General William Palmer lived from about 1781 till his death in 1816 with an aristocratic Muslim lady, Begum Faiz Baksh, and at the same time had a second bibi, a princess of Oudh. Clearly the pressure to be monogamous worked in only one direction. Charles Warre Malet was Resident at Poona when he lived with his bibi Amber Kaur and his children with her. The adventurers in Lucknow—Claude Martin, John Wombwell, and Colonel Antoine Polier—all amassed large fortunes by working for the East India Company, assumed immunity from British social norms, and perhaps drew their inspiration from prominent figures who did likewise. This group includes the artist Goerge Beechey, who lived in Lucknow with two or three unofficial Indian wives, and the diarist William Hickey who lived with Jemdanee for many years, till she died in childbirth.[2]

In this section, I study romance narratives for their articulations of English class and national aspirations, which are contested and challenged by the Indian lives of English men. Recent studies have emphasized the complex ways in which the colonial family was implicated in constructions of race, class, and ideas of legitimate authority. As Durba Ghosh points out, "the ways in which British men disciplined themselves and ordered their families gave rise to and crystallized widespread and deeply felt anxieties about the loss of class status, fears of racial degeneracy, and concerns about social acceptability" (Ghosh 14). The constitution of interracial families brought to the fore ideas about the legitimate and the sanctioned. British colonials were concerned about such relationships because they called for a redefinition of gender, class, and racial identity. Representations of Indian women and interracial domesticity are rare because of the illegitimacy of relationships of concubinage and other informal liaisons between British men and Indian women. However, the absence of Indian women in the colonial record should not be read as a sign of their historical and social inactivity. On the contrary, they "engaged with institutions of colonial governance as a way of negotiating financial provisions, gaining legal privileges, and expressing their cultural and religious affiliations, thereby making themselves subjects" (Ghosh 15–16). When they do appear, they are mentioned in legally recorded wills in which British men clearly articulated the relationships between themselves and their Indian companions, often transferred property to them, and made provision for the children from such marriages or relationships.[3] In the process, they outlined the ways in which they would like to be viewed by others; accounted for different kinds of personal and intimate connections that might not have been socially visible; and also constructed their lineage by arranging for the transfer of their names, property, and wealth.[4] By reading the wills of British men, court and church records, literary texts, biographies, and official and private correspondence, historians have given new substance to the silent and absent native women in the colonial archive.

Unexpectedly, portraits and paintings of the period also became a record of the close relationships between British men and their Indian wives and bibis. Mildred Archer, in her pioneering study of these portraits by European artists, identifies, for example, Charles Warre Malet's bibi Amber Kaur. Not surprisingly, she does not appear in Malet's official genealogy. James Wales's portrait of Amber Kaur shows a calm and composed woman "wearing rich jewellery studded with emeralds and pearls and swathed in a gauze sari" (Archer 340–41). She and Malet had three children, Eliza, Henry Charles, and Louisa, all of whom were christened in Bombay in 1797. Official history records that on his return to England, Malet married an Englishwoman, Susannah. He took his children by Amber Kaur with him and they were raised by Susannah with her own children by Malet (Archer 349). Malet left Amber Kaur at Poona, making sure that she was well provided for. In much the same way, Archer locates the bibi of another Lucknow European—probably Wombwell—through an interpretation of her portrait. Charles Smith, the Scottish painter, portrays her as a richly attired Muslim woman showing a calmness of mien and a confidence not associated with an orthodox Muslim woman of rank, who, in any case, would not have allowed herself to be painted in public. From the fact that she looks too relaxed to be a courtesan, Archer concludes that she was Wombwell's bibi (Archer 182). While some interracial relationships were temporary or experimental, Thomas Williamson reminds us that many had the same status as marriage:

> a woman "under the protection" of an European gentleman, is accounted, not only among the natives, but even by his countrymen to be equally sacred, as though she were married to him; and the woman herself values her reputation, exactly in proportion as she may have refrained from indulging in variety: some are said to have passed twenty years, or more, without the possibility for scandal to attach to their conduct.[5]

The easy crossing of racial boundaries, while it also expresses a relationship of patronage between the rulers and the ruled, clearly allowed the kind of social interaction that was to disappear in the next few decades.

There is no record from that period, however, which would explain how conservative Muslim women came to accept their positions as bibis of Englishmen and futures in which financial security was accompanied by the possibility of separation from children and the eventual breakup of the family. We do not hear, for instance, how Amber Kaur felt about being left in Poona, though it is assumed that the provisions made for her were satisfactory and that she accepted the separation from her children as part of the arrangement. Scattered references suggest that these women came from aristocratic families. While the privilege of birth gave them a certain freedom, it must surely have imposed restrictions on interaction with men of another race and culture. We learn nothing about the problems that had to be overcome for such relationships to be conducted over a long period of time.

In a rare instance of violent protest against colonial patriarchy and the pressures of interracial relationships, James Skinner, the founder of a cavalry regiment in the Indian army, records in his Persian memoir that:

> In the year 1790, my poor mother died, she could not endure that her two (younger) daughters should be forced from her and sent to school. She conceived that by their being taken away from her protection, the sanctity of the purdah was violated, and the Rajput honour destroyed; and, apprehensive of their disgracing themselves, from being removed from the care of all their female relatives contrary to the custom of the Rajputs, she put herself to death.[6]

In this self-destructive gesture, Skinner's mother asserted both her right to determine her daughters' upbringing, and her disapproval of the modernizing project of female education. In this episode, cultural syncretism seems a utopian ideal that conceals the clash of cultures and values. This snippet from late-eighteenth-century history hints at similar forces at work in the future cultural battles over the education, social roles, and emancipation of Indian women. Skinner's mother sees in her daughters not the product of a mixed marriage or the possibility of a hybrid cultural heritage, but symbols of Rajput honor. The happy family comes to a crisis on the question of those cultural values that the young girls are seen intrinsically to bear and those they might acquire.

Interracial relationships became possible in early colonial India perhaps because there were as yet no rigorous rules of conduct or strictly enforced segregation between the whites and the native population. Historians have described colonial society of this time as amorphous and not yet driven by the fierce desire for segregation. Some have identified this moment as coming after the "encounter" with a native population, but before the colonizing power becomes a "settler" community.[7] India was not meant to be a colony of settlement even though the number of whites there was comparable to that of many other settler colonies.

In the factory settlements of the seventeenth century in Surat, Bombay, Calcutta, and Madras, meals at the common table and a celibate lifestyle were the norm.[8] But at the beginning of the seventeenth century, Englishwomen were already being allowed to come to India, "partly to prevent illicit unions with country women and partly to lessen the temptation to marry Portuguese Roman Catholics" (Spear, "Nabobs" 13). There were, however, too few Englishwomen at this time to ward off the danger of mixed marriages.[9] While, on the one hand, the Company was concerned about the possibility of interracial or interreligious marriages, on the other, it also seems to have been the case that "there was no very lasting colour prejudice in the early eighteenth century, and marriage with coloured women was accepted as the normal course" (Spear, "Nabobs" 13). Sons of such marriages were also not discriminated against on the basis of color. On the whole, though, the incidence of such marriages was not very high.[10] Only after 1750, with the emergence of a more cosmopolitan culture in the cities, particularly in Calcutta, did marriages and informal arrangements between British officers and Indian women increase in number.

Between 1757 and 1780 many Company and army officers, independent adventurers and bohemian artists contracted informal liaisons with Indian women. In Calcutta, for instance, these decades saw the influx of a more varied European population. For young employees of the

Company, the chances of earning enough money to bring a wife from England were slim. Even most of the older officers were compelled to leave their wives and families in England because it was too expensive to maintain an establishment in India and to provide appropriate education for children. And even though India was considered a land of opportunity for single Englishwomen looking for husbands, men still outnumbered women.[11] This situation made arrangements with Indian women more viable and attractive.

Both in districts and in an urban center like Calcutta, relationships with Indian women meant that the nature of the domestic establishment changed. Unlike the prosperous merchant of the previous decades who quietly invested his money in land back home, affluent employees of the Company now wanted titles, grandeur, and social prominence. In the country districts, their establishments emulated those of the Muslim aristocracy. They styled themselves after the Nawabs of various states and enjoyed the same leisure activities as their titled allies. As many paintings of the period testify, watching "nautch" or dancing girls was one of these popular pastimes which often led to temporary associations between Englishmen and the dancers. Most long-term associations, though, were with upper-class Muslim women. This was only to be expected, given that the British had closer political and social links with the Muslim rather than Hindu aristocracy. Following Muslim tradition, many officers and independent Englishmen also adopted the custom of keeping a harem. Among a limited number of Company officers, a more lively interest in Indian culture meant the study of Persian literature or Hindu mythology. Orientalist learning had begun to flourish under the patronage of Warren Hastings, bringing a new respect for the classical cultures and traditions of India. All these factors added up to a unique cultural exchange that was recalled with nostalgia in the nineteenth century, when racial and cultural segregation was more rigorously enforced in English social circles.[12]

The general tolerance of these arrangements extended to the children of such unions. Prejudice against Eurasians, as children of mixed marriages were called, increased as the century progressed. One of the reasons for this increase in prejudice may have been the fact that after the last few decades of the eighteenth century, such mixed marriages were no longer an upper-class phenomenon. It was not difficult for the well-placed fathers of such children to use their contacts to find employment for their sons. The daughters, if they could pass for white, would have fairly good prospects for marriage. It was harder to provide for them if they could not pass, and they would then have to be trained in some profession. But without this privilege of class, such mixed children were condemned to be social and cultural pariahs. By the late eighteenth century, the care of these children began to present a serious administrative problem, and finally a military orphan society was formed in Calcutta in 1783. Earlier, such children had somehow been absorbed into the service of the Company as clerks or writers. In 1786, the Court of Directors objected to this practice, and in 1791, they went so far as to say that the illegitimate sons of British fathers and Indian mothers were ineligible for the service of the Company. Further, no Anglo-Indians could become sworn officers of the Company's ships between Europe and India (S. C. Ghosh 83). Clearly, as in other colonial contexts, intermarriage came to have serious social and political consequences for the British empire and needed to be managed. The fear that 'Eurasians' would constitute themselves into a political group in same manner as the mixed populations in the French Caribbean colony of Santo Domingo in 1790 led the Company to disperse this population and actively prevent them from being recognized as a distinct cultural-racial entity.[13] As it was, in 1830, Eurasians, under the leadership of John Ricketts, petitioned that they be treated as British subjects and not natives. The petition was heard in both houses of British Parliament but ultimately turned down. Financial troubles, a lack of leadership in the Eurasian community after the death of Ricketts in 1835, and the economic dependence of Eurasians on the Company probably led to a dispersal of any further political initiative.[14] In the mid- and late nineteenth century, the much-vaunted theories of racial superiority and the consequent closing of ranks against the native population were exacerbated further, according to some accounts, by the coming of the memsahibs (white European women) to India. Anglo-Indian relations became increasingly strained and some writers see a decisive break appearing with the Mutiny in 1857. With the nineteenth century came segregation and official disapproval, so that such liaisons between British men and Indian women were looked upon as major transgressions. In 1909, when Lord Crewe of the British colonial office issued a circular warning new recruits into the colonial service of the "disgrace and official ruin" which would certainly follow should they enter into "arrangements of concubinage with girls or women belonging to native populations" (Hyam, "Concubinage" 171), he was making official an unwritten prohibition on such liaisons that had been growing in strength since at least the middle of the nineteenth century.

Almost a third of such relationships were between British men and female servants.[15] So Archer's romantic history of interracial love in an elite section of Muslim and British society needs to be put into the larger perspective of such relationships in colonial India. Jenny Sharpe cautions us about reading a history of interracial relationships solely from this elite section of Muslim and British society by reminding us that "historically, the relationship between a British colonialist and his Indian mistress, or bibi, was no romantic love. Rather, she performed in the capacity of a servant who tended to her master's needs, including his sexual ones. The bibi was often (though not always) a village woman sold into prostitution as re-payment for family debts . . . the British did not destroy indigenous forms of the sex trade so much as incorporate them into modern colonialism" (Sharpe, "Figures" 159). Sharpe's comments are thus a salutary reminder of the wide range of circumstances within which interracial liaisons took place.

The question of "hybridity" inevitably comes up in any discussion of interracial relations. The extent and nature of the hybrid culture produced in colonial India have not been the focus of historical debates, and they are not the focus of *Educating Seeta* either. A strong argument for a kind of cultural syncretism comes from the art historian Mildred Archer, who believes that the years between 1786 and 1793 produced a kind of hybrid culture reflecting the class aspirations of the officials of the East India Company who lived like "nabobs."[16] She argues that at this time the social life of the Presidencies took on a new character, and while the emphasis on being British stayed, Englishmen wore Indian dress, enjoyed curries hot with chilies, smoked the hookah, and attended "nautches" (dances). I would argue, however, that insofar as hybrid culture usually suggests developments in language, cuisine, clothing, music, and other arts, there was no significant cultural manifestations of hybridity in colonial India.[17] A useful contrast with the Indian situation would be the Caribbean and Latin America, where racial and cultural hybridity has been central to discussions of identity and nationhood. One obvious reason for this is the pervasiveness of racial mixing and the large size of their mixed population. Despite this fact, colonial discourses of race and culture in Mexico, the Caribbean, and Latin America vilified 'La Malinche,' the progenitor of the race with the Spanish conquistadore Cortez, as a victim and collaborator who had betrayed the Indian people.[18] We have to credit anticolonial movements with reclaiming the term as politically valuable, as inaugurating a new era in our understanding of the formation of contemporary identities, and for taking stock of historical processes which brought about such hybridity. However, in Asia, racial mixing did not produce hybridity as a concept that was embraced and made politically efficacious by those whom it affected the most. In the colonial period, mixed Euro-Asian populations never became a visible or potent constituency. The numbers were comparatively small and informal patronage by European officials led to a dispersal and diffusion of mixed-race children who were produced during colonialism. This is not to say that there was not a distinctive Anglo-Indian population, in India for instance; it is rather to emphasize that it did not recognize itself as a political force, nor make sustained public claims as a distinct cultural group. A useful contrast would be with the French colony of Santo Domingo, where the Creole population did organize itself on those terms and constitute itself into a political constituency in the uprising of 1791.[19]

While my discussions of interracial romance are confined to upper-class British men and Indian women and the literary narratives that frame them, I resist a simple 'celebration' of romance, offering instead an analysis of the tropes of family as they encode moves of assimilation, collaboration, and resistance. The Anglo-Indian romance enables such a study because it is deeply involved with domestic life, which is made up in equal parts of fantasy, material reality, and politics. In the first chapter of this section, I show how domestic drama rather than the idea of "rescue and civilize" dominate the story of William Linneaus Gardner and his aristocratic Muslim wife with whom he raised a large family in a mixed household in North India in the early nineteenth century. Gardner's letters to his cousin Edward, written late in his life, after twenty-two years of marriage, describe an interracial relationship located in an upper-class milieu. As a counterpoint to the dominance of rescue narratives about Indian women, this episode from colonial history shows this Indian wife empowered in the home and responsible for initiating political and social alliances that consolidated the status of the family. In this version of interracial romance, I study class compacts that make cultural crossings easy: Gardner's lifestyle mixes upper-class Muslim with English interests and habits, a fact that he alternately embraces and resists.

The second chapter is about interracial romances written in the early twentieth century. Even though historians have generally understood this period as one of greater segregation between the British and Indians and hence less conducive to interracial relationships, romancers return to the subject compulsively, often harking back to the heyday of such relationships in the late eighteenth century. Thus, though separated by roughly a century and a half from the historical period of interracial romances, early-twentieth-century women romancers nonetheless thematically invoke them. I focus on the romances of Bithia Mary Croker, especially her *In Old Madras* (1913), which dwells with horrified fascination on interracial love and mixed households. The popularity of Croker's romances raises many questions about what readers wanted to imagine and experience in Britain's encounter with India. *In Old Madras*, in particular, leads them through vicarious pleasure in observing mixed marriages and households outside of official Anglo-Indian culture. At the core of the romance lies a heroic tale of rescue, but it seems driven more by the various interracial domestic arrangements it unearths, which serve as a dramatic and Gothic foil to the rather pallid love between an Englishman and English woman.

CHAPTER ONE

"Half an Asiatic"
William Linnaeus Gardner and Anglo-Muslim Domesticity

English accounts of relationships with Indian women usually imagine them as tales of rescue in which benevolent Englishmen save Indian women from distressing situations such as forced marriage, inconsiderate relatives, or worst of all, the injunction to commit Sati with their dead husbands. The idea of rescuing Indian women from indigenous practices, customs, men, and oppressive families expresses nicely British benevolence and civilizational superiority. For British writers, describing these interracial relationships as "rescue" narratives keeps British respectability and civility intact and makes honor and love the motivating forces for British men. I argue here, however, that the domestic realities of negotiating a mixed household and parenting half-Indian children far exceed the rescue narrative. Instead of British benevolence, we see a class compact between an Englishman and his Indian wife in which the complex negotiations of domestic and cultural power are played out in a mixed household.

The romance of empire produces a fantasy in which the native woman becomes an ally of the colonizer and is gradually educated into becoming the perfect subject and wife. My larger argument in this book is that Indian women presented the recalcitrant element that would not be assimilated into this colonial fantasy. The domestic arrangements and mixed household of William Linneaus Gardner (1772–1835) and his aristocratic Muslim wife, Mah Munzalool nissa Begum, show that it is the Englishman who gets acculturated to a North Indian upper-class Muslim lifestyle. The colonial romance we get is not about the successful education, conversion, and rescue of the native woman by an Englishman. Instead, Gardner's wife can be seen in the midst of a primarily Muslim household, active in organizing ceremonies and rituals related to the marriage of her children, and participating in decisions about their education. Her influence also extends beyond the home, and the cultural and economic capital she brings with her consolidates the social status of her husband. As Gardner represents the details of his domestic life, he comes across as a man who, while accepting some Indian acculturation, continues to assert his English identity. But two generations later, Gardner's grandson, having adopted an aristocratic Muslim lifestyle, became a famous and prolific poet writing in Urdu and Persian under the name "Fana."

My account of William Linneaus Gardner's domestic life is based on the letters he wrote to his cousin, Edward Gardner, which are the only available record of his life. Between January 5, 1820 and December 23, 1821, Gardner wrote 120 letters to his cousin, who was the British Resident in Nepal.[1] Much of the original bound collection of letters has been damaged by water, but fortunately a typed transcript from some time before 1963 is available. From this source, I have tried to construct those scenes from Gardner's life that suggest the kind of social power Indian women could assume in an interracial household.[2]

Letters assume a special significance in the eighteenth and nineteenth centuries, when there was "a culture of sensibility" in which private feelings and emotions could be expressed by both men and women. Connections with home and family overseas, links with other British men similarly positioned in India, and informal communication about social and political matters were carried on in letters. Kate Teltscher makes a case for the significance of the letter as a colonial document when she writes that, "mediating between periphery and the metropolis, the exotic and the domestic, the spheres of work and home, the familiar letter was central to the construction of colonial identity" (Teltscher 282). I argue in this chapter that Gardner keeps alive his sense of his English identity in his letters to his cousin. His ironic and humorous comments about his Indian life express both a level of comfort with it, but also some distance from it when his English values and ideas dominate. Because these letters were written towards the end of Gardner's life (he died in 1835), they provide an opportunity for him to reflect on a wide range of interests and preoccupations. With Edward,

Gardner he shares gossip about peers, information about family and social events, financial worries, and reflections on his life.

I place Gardner's life in the context of late-eighteenth- and early-nineteenth-century India by presenting parallel examples from the life of James Achilles Kirkpatrick, a contemporary of Gardner and Resident in the South Indian state of Hyderabad, whose marriage to the aristocratic Khair-un-nissa and the context in which it took place have been narrated so evocatively and comprehensively by William Dalrymple in his *White Mughals*. The private papers of both Gardner and Kirkpatrick provide glimpses of a mixed household, an English lifestyle grafted on to a predominantly Muslim one, and male friendship and camaraderie with English men in a world segregated from their romantic relationships with Indian women. Their sense of the superiority of British civilization combines with an uneasy recognition of the value of their Indian wives. In each case, the courtship and marriage have all the elements of a medieval tale of romance in which the glimpse of a beautiful maiden elicits the appropriately chivalrous response from the English hero while his potential as her savior makes him irresistible to the maiden. On further examination, however, we get a more complex picture of a new aristocratic elite, both British and Muslim, who share and maintain cultural and political power. More importantly, Gardner's tale begins with a rescue narrative, but departs from it because in their long married life his wife retains the kind of cultural power not attained by the ultimately abandoned and tragic figure of Kirkpatrick's Khair-un-nissa. Gardner's wife, like many other eighteenth-century Indian bibis, or informal wives of British colonials, was also a critical source of information about language, culture, social structures, and power relations. Chris Bayly notes this phenomenon of late-eighteenth-century India when he writes that "women had always been central to the process of faction and alliance building in India" (Bayly 91).

Colonel William Linneaus Gardner, who is best known for training a body of distinguished military cavalry corps called "Gardner's Horse," arrived in India at a very young age seeking the exotic delights of the East through employment in the army. He was employed by the Maratha ruler Tukoji Holkar for whom he trained an infantry unit. After Tukoji's death, Gardner continued working for his successor, Yashwant Rao Holkar. Gardner was stationed with his corps at Khassgunge in 1819, at Saugor in 1821, at Bareilly in 1821–23, in Arracan in 1825, and at Khassgunge again in 1826–27. After 1828, Gardner does not appear in the British or Indian army lists.[3] As his letters show, he had decided to retire and disperse his corps. He established himself as a *zamindar* (landlord) in Khasgunge in Uttar Pradesh, and lived there in a predominantly Muslim household with his wife, the Nawab Mah Munzalool nissa Begum Dheline, daughter of the Nawab of Cambay. Gardner's letters are a record of his interests, anxieties, political concerns, and hopes for himself and his family; they also provide glimpses of the mixed Indian Muslim and English domestic life of this interracial couple.

From 1820 to the time he died, Gardner seems to have been consumed by his financial concerns and desire to leave the army. The East India Company refused to recognize him as an officer of the British army and despite his commission considered him a "Mahratta officer." This angered Gardner, who was facing both the reduction of his corps and supersession by a junior officer. At the urging of the then Governor-General, the Marquess of Hastings, he petitioned the Prince Regent to retain his proper rank in the military. Feeling let down by the Marquis, Gardner wrote, "I am disgusted with the Service" (16 Nov. 1820), and "I feel a foolish sort of Pride that I have acted uprightly in my Command, and have founded my Claims on the Approbation of Government on my services and the fidelity with which I have served them" (5 March 1820). Like many independent English adventurers of an earlier era, he was horrified at the aggressive and hostile policies of the British rulers towards India. Dalrymple, in his account of the romance of Kirkpatrick and Khair-un-nissa, reports a similar falling out between James Kirkpatrick and Governor-General Wellesley (1797–1805) over the question of just negotiations with Indian rulers.[4] Kirkpatrick also felt that the era of aggressive expansion inaugurated by Wellesley had led to dishonorable and unnecessarily cruel British policies. Dalrymple describes Gardner as the last survivor of a world in which "the relationship between India and Britain was a symbiotic one (Dalrymple xli). We can reasonably conclude that the political perspectives of Gardner and Kirkpatrick had been formed by their intimate Indian relationships.

Gardner had spent his early years in America and France. Colonel Lionel Gardner, his biographer and living descendant, writes that an adolescent William Linneaus, who lived in Paris with his mother, Alida, was fascinated by the lore of India brought back to France by French army officers and their Indian wives.[5] His admiration for these wives arose from the fact that they had "shy ways and a languid grace" he had not seen in any European women (Gardner 9). His French girlfriends apparently retaliated by describing the behavior of the Indian women as "smacking of the servility of slaves" (Gardner 9). Gardner insisted that their docility showed, in fact, love and respect for their husbands, "qualities sadly lacking in European wives" (Gardner 9). These conservative and patriarchal views of a young adolescent grew strong in the adult Gardner, who opposed the French revolution and criticized "old England and its revolutionary ladies." Gardner's life and career in India instantiates the eighteenth-century British vision of India as a place enabling chivalric deeds and grand gestures of honor in the manner of medieval knights and crusaders—a kind of premodern Eden untouched by the sociopolitical unrest that marked late-eighteenth- and early-nineteenth-century Europe.

In 1815, Gardner complained in a letter to his aunt that he had not heard from his family in England for seventeen years, in fact, ever since he announced his marriage to an Indian girl. Giving a brief account of his romance, he writes that in 1798, "I by accident saw the daughter, [of the Nawab of Kambay] when about fourteen years of age, and what originated in humanity and pity at my age [of 26] soon gave place to other sentiments, and I was soon after united to the lady with all the ceremonies, which by their religion were alone considered binding."[6] Gardner's marriage to an Indian woman also radically altered his relationship to his mother country, something that had always been understood as an unvarying condition of nostalgia and yearning for home. In the same letter, he wrote, "England appeared to me of all places the one in which I should be most a stranger, and the very idea of ever visiting it has now been long obliterated from my mind." Gardner's story is not an isolated incident. The many reports of a group of renegade army officers who lived with Indian women in the late eighteenth century captured the imagination of Victorian and Anglo-Indian writers, and until recently, these stories continued to provide the model for "Raj" stories.

Gardner's letter to his aunt describes a well-known narrative of a helpless young native girl granted protection by the European officer culminating in a marriage between the two. In a parallel example, Dalrymple speculates on how James Kirkpatrick was granted access to Khair-un-nissa, whose family were connected to the aristocratic prime minister of the Nawab of Hyderabad.[7] From the multiple sources available, one of the narratives that inevitably emerges is that the young Khair-un-nissa, wanting to escape from a hateful marriage arranged for her by her father, throws herself at Kirkpatrick. Describing their first meeting, Kirkpatrick writes that Khair-un-nissa expressed "a passion which I could not I confess help feeling myself something more than pity for."[8] Most Englishmen is such situations seem to have become benevolent saviors of hapless adolescent girls in a popular rescue narrative.

However, Gardner's letters show a tale that begins as a rescue narrative, but develops into a story about the power and prestige that aristocratic Muslim women brought to their interracial relationships. These women ruled their households and exercised considerable autonomy in practicing their religion and perpetuating the cultural practices of upper-class Muslims.

Fanny Parkes, in her autobiographical account, *Wanderings of a Pilgrim in Search of the Picturesque*, describes a meeting with the elderly Colonel Gardner in which he recounts for her the story of his marriage to the princess of Cambay. While in the employ of Tukoji Holkar, a young Gardner is sent to Cambay to negotiate a treaty. The young daughter of the Nawab, veiled and segregated but present at the court, out of a curiosity about the dashing young Englishman, pulls aside the corner of a curtain and looks at Gardner as he presents himself before the Nawab. Gardner sees "the most beautiful black eyes in the world" and promptly falls in love with her. He is so smitten that "it was impossible to think of the treaty; those bright and piercing glances, those beautiful dark eyes, completely bewildered me" (qtd. in Parkes 417). At the next meeting, he was anxious to see her again, and when "the parda again was gently moved, . . . my fate was decided" (qtd. in Parkes 417). He "demands" the princess's hand in marriage, but also warns the Nawab that if any attempt is made to marry him off to someone else in place of his daughter, he would declare open war. At first, the relations of the princess were positively indignant, but according to Gardner, his position as ambassador made them reluctant to thwart him, and perhaps, they also saw the marriage as an advantageous political alliance. At the wedding ceremony, Gardner lifted her veil and recognized the princess from her eyes! They were married according to Muslim ritual and established a domestic life which seemed predominantly Muslim. Gardner's romance with his wife is cast in the most Orientalist of terms as the repetition of the words "black eyes" shows. The erotics of the gaze, so much celebrated in cultures where there is segregation between men and women, is foregrounded in his memory of the encounter with the alluring "black eyes" of which he catches a mere glimpse.

When a report bordering on the scandalous appeared in a newspaper, Gardner wrote a rejoinder explaining how he came to be married to an Indian woman. In his letter, he denied the aura of romance that attaches to his marriage, saying that his wife was then only thirteen years old: "I fear I must divest my marriage with her highness the Begum of a great part of its romantic attraction, by confessing that the young Begum was only thirteen years of age when I first applied for and received her mother's consent" (qtd. in Parkes 415). Given that Gardner's response to the young princess was entirely in accordance with traditions of romance, it is difficult to understand what he meant by "divesting" his relationship with her of any romance. He seems to have thought of it as a hot-blooded and impulsive act, which he nevertheless lived by for the rest of his life. Many years later, on a visit to the Gardner estate, a bemused Fanny Parkes, watching the games and frivolous rituals attendant upon a Muslim marriage, asked the Colonel how he could have tolerated such folly at his own wedding. He responded by pointing out that "I was young then and in love, I would have done or promised anything" (qtd. in Parkes 439).

In his letter Gardner responds to the speculation in the newspaper article "that it is difficult to say what sort of bridal contract is gone through between a Moslem beauty and a Christian gentleman, but the ceremony is supposed to be binding" (qtd. in Parkes 412) with the observation that "a Moslem lady's marriage with a Christian, by a Cazee, is as legal in this country as if the ceremony had been performed by the Bishop of Calcutta; a point lately settled by my son's marriage with the niece of the Emperor, the Nawab Mulka Humanee Begum" (qtd. in Parkes 415). The cultural capital that attended such a marriage ensured its respectability and also gave it social and political power. In the same letter, Gardner also emphasizes that his granddaughters were brought up Christian by a special request of their grandmother even though the marriage contract had stipulated that the girls would be raised Muslim. He mentions this with an element of pride, thereby giving the lie to the possibility that he had shed his prejudice against Muslim acculturation. Gardner's devotion to his wife is further evident in the fact that in his will he leaves all his property and assets to her, and enjoins his son as executor to make sure that she is provided for.[9]

Not all brewing 'scandals' had such a happy ending, however. Here again the comparison with Kirkpatrick is instructive. Public scandals usually created a confrontation between official British values and the private lives of European men in India. In the case of Kirkpatrick and Khair-un-nissa, the relationship began in secret, though with the support of Khair-un-nissa's grandmother, but soon got embroiled in the ongoing political intrigues and power struggles at the court of the Nawab of Hyderabad. The hawkish Governor-General Wellesley strongly disapproved of the relationship and was alarmed at the charges of sexual coercion that had been brought against Kirkpatrick by court factions who were hostile to him. Kirkpatrick was then at pains to disprove these charges and to exonerate himself to the Governer-General, whose aggressive political attitude and behavior had already alienated Kirkpatrick from him. James's brother William, a high ranking official in the Company, interceded on his behalf, and though Kirkpatrick was finally able to make the case that his marriage was honorable, his career never showed the same promise as before.[10] Lt.-Colonel Gardner had better luck when he offered written clarification that his marriage had been recognized by the family of the Mughal king of Delhi (though now ruling only in name). He is something of an exception to the rule that interracial relationships were covert. The high social standing of his wife could be one reason why he felt comfortable acknowledging his relationship to her. For the women's families, contracting an alliance with a powerful ruling class could only produce positive results. This would explain not only why the immediate families of Gardner's Begum and Khair-un-nissa did not oppose their marrying Englishmen but in fact actively supported the idea. Both controversies raise piquant questions about the relationship between public profiles and private lives, the chivalric and romantic terms in which interracial relationships were defended, the culturally mixed lives led by these men, and most significantly, the presence of these women in their lives.

The kind of cultural syncretism practiced by elite Muslim families and independent Englishmen is the defining quality of late-eighteenth-century Anglo-Indian relations. Gardner seems to have known Urdu and may well have had knowledge of Persian. But for a man who lived all his life as part of a mixed household, which included at least two religions, cultures, and languages, he held to some colonial ideas in wanting his children to marry English Christians. This could, of course, be read as a comment about the crumbling fortunes of the Mughals and Muslim aristocracy in general rather than an expression of a colonial attitude about British superiority. The newspaper report cited above continues its somewhat scurrilous interest in the complexion of Gardner's daughter, and speculates about whether they were happy to be raised Muslim or chafed against the confinement that came with such an upbringing. It characterizes Gardner as "half an Asiatic" because he has passed most of his time adopting "the opinions and ideas" of Indians. It does not, however, refer to Gardner in any but the most respectful terms, despite his unorthodox lifestyle.

Gardner's openness about racial mixing signals a pre-Victorian consciousness in which race had not yet been loaded with the pseudoscientific language of biological evolution. His comments about race show that he connects them to class rather than biology. The word hybridity as referring to 'miscegenation' or interracial marriage has a particularly

Victorian lineage, and at least in literary texts, always carries allegorical potential.[11] I have already presented some historical reasons why interracial marriage and mixed children did not have a large presence in India. For literary treatments of the subject, it is de rigeur to turn to Kipling's short stories and *Kim* and I do so now to provide a contrast between Gardner's narrative and a canonical representation of miscegenation even though almost a century separates the life and writings of the two men. In his fine study of Kipling, John McBratney points out that even in someone as sympathetic to India as Kipling, the attitude towards Eurasians was that they were "caught between British and Indian societies, fundamentally inferior to both, and embraced by neither" (McBratney 55). This would explain the absence of narrative scripts that would include Eurasians as a central part of a literary plot. Late in the nineteenth century, the fear and repulsion against biological crossing and its perceived connection with degeneracy and moral and physical debility generated by the writings of Robert Knox, Count Gobineau, and Edward Long created a severe resistance to imagining children of mixed marriages or the consequences of interracial desire.[12] McBratney makes a telling distinction between 'mingling' and 'mixing': the first denotes a combination of two separate elements that keep their integrity intact while the second alters and transforms the two into a third entity (McBratney 63). While in *Kim,* Kipling can imagine a *cultural* mixing in Kim's ability to speak Indian languages and pass as Indian, he still cannot contemplate making him *racially* anything but white, and Irish at that. Making him racially mixed would have meant that "the 'pure' Briton is irretrievably lost within the Indian" (McBratney 64). A similar fear is at work in the representation of Indian women in Kipling's "Beyond the Pale," where "in the colonizer's hysterical imagination, a dangerously erotic female India . . . threatens to entomb Englishmen in an underworld from which they cannot return" (McBratney 71). This is still very much the landscape of adventure and romance in which racially other female figures threaten English values. Marriage and children cannot be accommodated in this imagination. My definition of 'family romance,' on the other hand, moves the discussion away from a Gothic register to the concerns of domesticity and the mundane and everyday challenges of organizing a household and the raising of children.

Gardner's letters reveal a very different kind of cultural experience from the English experience portrayed in Kipling's stories. He confronts racial mixing constantly, in his household, in his children, and his dependents. His affection for his family is expressed over and over again—he is afraid of being transported to England "from comfort and family" (16 Nov. 1820), and "how I long for Khassgunge—the Butchas [children]—the library, garden and liberty!" (26 Dec. 1820). On returning to his household in Khassgunge and his grandchildren, Gardner writes, "The shouts of joy when I return after an absence of any time can be heard for a mile. And the house is filled with Brats, and the very thinking of them, from Blue eyes and fair hair to Ebony and Wool makes me quite anxious to get back." (6 Jan. 1821). When he visited the home of James Skinner—another Anglo-Indian known for his mixed household and his Indian wife—Gardner notes that he saw "all Skinner's children of all hues and colors" (22 June 1820).

In a world where all manner of formal and informal alliances between English men and Indian women are common, Gardner's son James enters into a relationship with Mrs De Caneiro (who is most likely a Catholic of Portuguese descent), who is then accommodated in the Gardner household. Mrs De Canerio's two young daughters add to the already large number of young women in the household. Gardner's response to this is definitely couched in racial terms as becomes clear from this letter laced with his usual riqué humor, when he writes to Edward: "I have now 12 girls of European blood, under 14 years of age, to provide for and get married, how and to whom, God knows. Will you have two or three?" (9 March 1821). While social status seems to have been the paramount consideration in arranging marriages, race was certainly considered. All Gardner's daughters married Englishmen so that their status would be secured while the sons had the flexibility to marry Indian women. Yet race is only considered in terms of class and status. There is no reflection on its connection to physical strength, morality, or other human capacities. I would argue that in Gardner's letter, race gets almost entirely subsumed under culture, class, and religion. From the evidence of his letters and the example of other Englishmen in his situation, the same kind of acceptance of racial mixing prevailed among his peers. And, among this small group of elite families in late-eighteenth- and early-nineteenth-century India who lived in Anglo-Muslim households, English husbands, while strenuously insisting on English values, were nevertheless competent in Indian language, idioms, customs, and manners. The hybrid self that Gardner does not acknowledge to Edward nevertheless comes through in his smooth and unselfconscious use of language that is replete with Urdu and Hindustani words such as 'butchas' (children), 'pukowing' (cooking), 'dada' (grandfather), 'zillah' (district), 'goulam' (slave), 'takraar' (quarrel), 'nuzzur' (sighting), and 'mungnee' (engagement).

Fanny Parkes gives a vivid description of the Gardner household, and also the home of his son James, who married into a branch of the ruling Mughals of Delhi. In her account, Gardner appears as a gallant old man trying to keep his family together and battling financial worries. She reports on the power of the women within the household, and their active participation in making decisions about their children's education and marriages. "I fancy the Begum, his mother, would never hear of her son's going to England for education . . . " (Parkes 436). Parkes's understanding of "native" women leads her to conclude that through a display of anger and sulkiness, they would have got their way in most such decisions. Hence, when the Begum did not want James to go to England for education like many other mixed-race children, her wishes carried the day.[13] The Begum follows the injunctions laid down for upper-class Muslim women by actively donating money for religious causes. Parkes notes that "the sums of money and the quantity of food distributed by Colonel Gardner's Begum in charity was surprising; she was a religious woman, and fulfilled, as far as was in her power, the ordinances of her religion" (Parkes 436). The Begum did not lack initiative when it came to financial matters either. Her son James tried to buy land in a village, but could not complete the deal because the East India Company had just passed new regulations prohibiting foreigners from buying land. The Begum wrote triumphantly to Gardner that she immediately sent an application for purchase of the land in her own name (he uses the word "dhurkchaust" or appeal) "certifying that she was not a feringhy butcha [child of foreigners]" and got the land within the village. Although Gardner's response to this is to make misogynistic remarks about the growing power of women, there is grudging admiration as well. Parkes's comments on the old Begum's daughter-in-law are even more complimentary. William Gardner's son, James Gardner, a local landowner who runs an indigo farm, is assisted in his business by the advice of his wife, Mulka Begum, "to whom the natives look up with highest respect" (Parkes 436). Mulka Begum's power and charisma extend beyond her own household, and "her word is regarded as law by her villagers and dependents" (Parkes 436). James Gardner's wife may have brought these villages in her dowry or may have exercised power over the villagers because of her connection with the royal family of Delhi, but it is clear that as a married woman, she continued to exercise her inherited social power.

In such a household, Gardner often comes across as a compliant and long-suffering husband who accedes to all the demands of the women. When an English gentleman inquires through Parkes if Gardner would be willing to give him his granddaughter in marriage, he responds, "Tell Mr—— I am flattered by his wish to be of my family, and would willingly give him my grand-daughter, but the Begum is bent on this *grand alliance,* as *she* considers it" (Parkes 396; emphasis in original). Gardner is referring to the Begum's insistence that their granddaughter marry a young prince of Delhi. The negotiations for his son James's wedding are vividly presented in Gardner's usual satiric tone. Writing from Ourvowdah, on the left bank of the Jumna, five miles from Calpee, he says, " . . . The Begum is settling her abominable marriage with Sombres Begum[14] for James, and I do not expect her to return till the end of May unless she gets jealous of the slave girls at Khassgunge" (34). His tongue-in-cheek remarks throughout his letters underscore the quiet domestic felicity achieved after a long, happy marriage. Gardner's anxiety about his financial situation pervades the letters and James's impending marriage brings it out again. But attached to this concern is also a commitment to his wife as this comment shows: "I fear James's marriage will make a deep hole in the 15,000 but n'importe, the marriage will be Hindostanee, and it would break the Mother's heart not to have Kettle Drum and fireworks" (13 July 1821). The Begum dominates the proceedings as Gardner makes clear:

> I believe James is to be contracted at the next Eid [Muslim festival] but can say nothing certain as I am not in the secret—and women are going between daily and the business appears something like the National Debt and sinking fund for I understand as much of the one as of the other—my part is prompted and I act it as instructed—all I have had to do as yet was to tell the old Begum [Samroo] I had brought her a goulam [slave]. Her answer was you have brought my eyes and liver!! This I am told is all as it should be—the only thing I have interfered in was to place my veto to the whole Royal Family coming to the shadee [marriage] as I can not afford it. (6 June 1820)

Gardner explains tongue-in-cheek that the women plot and negotiate a marriage for his son, while he is left out of it all entirely until "prompted." He plays his part gamely by engaging in witty repartee with the old Begum, who makes protestations of deep affection for his wife, her "slave." Only when it comes to financial matters does he put his foot down and refuse to invite the entire royal family to the wedding.

During the negotiations for his son James's wedding in Delhi, Gardner observes that the Begum Samroo "so mixes Hindoostanee and Christian" custom that the British Resident David Ochterlony and

Gardner were both pressed into service to find precedents or invent a mourning ceremony combining both kinds of rituals to mark the death of the Begum's relative, Mrs Dyce. This episode provides insight into the syncretic cultural universe that Gardner occupied, though he sounds more long-suffering than an active participant. However, it must be noted that most of his complaints are about the expense involved in feeding hundreds of people and the impatience of an older man being conscripted into ceremonies and rituals for which he seems to have only the most perfunctory regard. When the irresponsible Ochterlony forgets about this ceremony, Gardner becomes anxious that "the ceremony and expense will devolve on me in the character of sumdee [relative], and costs from 3 to 4000 Rs in dresses to the family and feeding. Not only her large family but to the wives and families of all the great folks of Delhi who have taken up their quarters at her House from the Day of Mrs D's Death" (7 July 1820). In his next letter, Gardner explains that James's intended is the daughter of Mrs Dyce, and hence the family is placed in the awkward position of being in mourning while planning a wedding. Ochterlony finally agrees to the ceremony of the Soogh, a ceremonial observance for a mourning in the family, which involves holding a feast for the extended family and others connected to the estate of Begum Sumroo. Gardner hints that this matter would not be resolved without squabbling between the Begum and Ochterlony, presumably on the subject of expenses. His lively report on the activities in a household which is in the midst of planning an engagement also reveals the central role of women in cultural and social activities. The intermingling of Christian and Muslim custom seems to be an accepted part of this small group of elite families who had intermarried.

Images of the "mixed" life that Gardner led also filter through in his discussion of his library and garden, surely the most British of institutions (although here reflective equally of a Muslim fascination with ornamental gardens), and his large extended family follows the tradition of country estates among the Indian aristocracy. Stationed at Saugor, he writes to Edward, "How I long for Khassgunge—the Butchas—the library, garden and liberty!"(26 Dec. 1820). A similar interest in gardens as an expression of British identity can be found in the case of James Kirkpatrick. His longing for England can be gleaned from the fact that he acquired farmland in which "he wished to create the sort of gentle, informal park that William Kent, Capability Brown and Humphrey Repton had made fashionable in the England of his youth: an arrangement that had become as central to British conceptions of peaceful, civilized refinement, as cool rippling waters and the shade of overarching broadleaf trees was to that of the Mughals" (Dalrymple 332). It was not the most successful of experiments. What visitors to the Residency remembered were extensive gardens "principally Indian in inspiration" (Dalrymple 333). Fanny Parkes notes that Gardner, like his godfather William Linneaus, is "an excellent botanist. . . . [H]is garden at Khasgunge is a very extensive and most delightful one" and that "it is one of the pleasures of the Begum and her attendants to spend the day in that garden" (Parkes 397). Among the rare trees and plants are many with medicinal properties. In Parkes's words, the Begum, "although not a botanist, after the European fashion, . . . knows the medicinal qualities of all the Indian plants, and the dyes that can be produced from them; and this knowledge is of daily account in the zenana" (Parkes 397). Both Gardner and his Begum seem to have found a harmonious co-existence based on different systems of beliefs.

In another instance of mixed traditions in his life, Gardner's belief in European systems of medicine co-exists with his acceptance of the efficacy of indigenous Indian remedies. He reports in a letter to Edward that his Begum is keeping in reasonably good health, but though the Dhilimichi (an honorific for his wife) is happy and for the present does not feel her illness . . . I think unless she submits to European treatment her life is a very bad one" (1 August 1820). Yet later in the month, when he had an attack of cholera which became so serious that he was rendered "cold and insensible," the family physician Dr. Scott, "was obliged to resign his situation of Doctor to the Begum" (28 Aug. 1820). She takes charge and in Gardner's wry narration pours down his throat "such a mixture of black and red pepper, garlic juice, onion juice, and ginger juice as was enough to have embalmed an Egyptian" (28 Aug. 1820). There is no evidence to suggest that this incident converted Gardner to another system of medicine or that he acknowledged the limitations of European cures. However, he did not refuse herbal cures and certainly supported his wife in her pursuit of such cures.

This does not of course present a case for religious and cultural hybridity because even though Gardner was constantly surrounded by different customary and religious practices, he expresses great irreverence for religion, especially Catholicism, Islam, and Hinduism. In the absence of any connection with organized religion or a community, he shows an acceptance of different customs, but not necessarily an appreciation of them. He is particularly satirical about Hindu practices that he encounters. Some of this satire is also caused by the fact that these practices are found in his newly appointed senior, General Stuart. Unexpectedly, General Stuart relishes Hindu rituals and Gardner speculates that "he does not pride himself on the capacity of his stomach or the strength of his head as he regularly performs his poojah [Hindu prayer] and avoid the sight of beef" (5 Jan. 1820). Later the General invites Gardner to meet him at the bathing ghats (steps) of the river where Hindus bathe and then leaves him in command of the corps while he visits a Hindu temple. Gardner reports that he greets every Hindu with "jhey sittaramjee" (Hail to Ram and Sita). Even more amusing is the report that General Stuart "was riding around the Cantonment this morning seated behind his Pundit [priest] on a camel!" (4 April 1820). In another letter to Edward, Gardner writes about Hindu bathing rituals believed to wash off all sins. The occasion for these remarks is the fact that his "Hindoo fellows" have been insisting that they want to go and bathe in the river "Nerbudda" (Narmada) because such an auspicious conjunction of planets would not happen again for 2500 years. Gardner writes, "What a charming religion! This and the Roman Catholic Apostolic Church are the only comfortable ones after all. Our somber adoration gives the National tone—see how blithe and gay the French and Italians are. No wonder when weekly absolution balances all accounts" (28 March 1821).

Despite his somewhat typical responses to religious practice, and his long-suffering response to the expense involved, however, it is clear that in the Gardner household Muslim festivals are celebrated with expense and traditional pomp. In a letter dated September 19, Gardner writes: "I was in hopes to have avoided the noise and expense of a Khassgunge Ede, but here are all the Widows (?) of the country come to torment me. . . . So God bless you, I could not consider the Ede as Ede had I not assured you, my dear Edward, how affectionately I am yours." We can guess from these remarks that Gardner accepts the Muslim festival of Id as a festive occasion and probably participated in the festivities. On the other hand, the Muslim festival of Muharram does not seem to have been a favorite of his. His comments about it are noteworthy for the episode they describe involving his irreverent half-brother Valentine, whose behavior seems to have worried Gardner for the latter part of his life. Announcing the upcoming festival, Gardner writes, "My torment, the Mohurrum, has commenced. . . . Val was allowed to look at the sanctum sanctorum last night, on the promise of good behavior, which he kept, with the exception of spanking his backside in sympathy with the maatam (mourning)! However, as he managed these responsive beats without the Begum's seeing him, it all passed very well" (10 Oct. 1820). So even though he doesn't participate in the observances, Gardner is concerned that his wife not be angered by any show of irreverence for one of the most important occasions for Shia Muslims in which the martyrdom of Hussein, the grandson of the Prophet, at Karbala, is remembered with acts of mourning and commemoration. At any given time, Gardner's household is composed of outsiders and observers as much as enthusiastic participants in Muslim ceremonies. Gardner is thus placed in the strange position of openly acknowledging his discomfort with Muslim ritual yet being embarrassed by an outright act of disrespect for the religion of his wife. Sharing his concern about arranging suitable marriages for his daughters, granddaughters, and other young female relatives in his extended family, rather coarsely expressed as "providing for the blood fillies," Gardner muses, "what would people say if it was known that they are not Christians, nor are they pagans, still less have I had them circumcised" (Letter 70). Dalrymple's speculations about a comparable situation, the mixed household of Khair-un-nissa and James Kirkpatrick, are instructive here. He notes Khair's piety and concludes that she must have wanted her children to be raised as Muslims. Kirkpatrick could have no objections to this as he had been willing to undergo a formal conversion ceremony so that he could marry her. Dalrymple notes that, though "there is no unequivocal evidence that he regularly practiced his new faith, or regarded himself as a an active Muslim, his mother-in-law, who lived closely with him, certainly believed him to be such, as did his Munshi, Aziz Ullah" (Dalrymple 340). Neither Gardner nor Kirkpatrick really discusses what the proximity to Muslim practices meant to them. Dalrymple mentions the fact that Gardner converted to Islam to marry his Begum,[15] but their "official" life required them to assume and perform an English persona and uphold English values. Thus, though the evidence shows their relative comfort and ease with a Muslim lifestyle, it is hard to make a case for a hybrid or syncretic culture in which both kinds of cultural and religious practices were harmoniously blended. It was, rather, more a case of peaceful co-existence.

In navigating the difficult waters of cultural influence and indoctrination, Gardner was very concerned about reproducing British masculinity in his sons. He seems to have been unhappy with his son James's affair with Mary de Caniero, a Eurasian widow who sought Gardner's protection. Gardner claims, in one of his letters, that since he considers her under his protection, he is particularly unhappy about James's paying court to her. James's second marriage was similarly marked by scandal at the court of Oudh, the Mughal court, and in Gardner's family. Gardner offered protection to Mulka Begum, the niece of the Mughal emperor who was visiting her sister, the wife of the King of Oudh. The

King fell in love with her and wanted to marry her against her will. At her father's behest, Gardner persuaded the King to give her up and brought her into his large household. While she was living in his home, Gardner's son James fell in love with her and they eloped. Gardner was so unhappy with his son that he refused to speak to him for two years. At the end of that period, James appealed to him and Gardner finally softened his hard stand on the issue. He seems to have been very unsympathetic towards his son's romantic aspirations which were compounded by the "dishonorable" manner in which he acted upon them. James seems to have acted honorably in the end, however. In his will, he left most of his property and assets to his wife Mulka Begum, but also provided for his mistress Mary de Caniero and acknowledged his children by her.[16]

Beleagured and disaffected as he was towards the end of his life, Gardner emphatically states again and again that his greatest happiness was in being with his family. Discussing his plans for retiring from his corps to his estate in Khasgunge, he writes about his finances, his desire for a more settled and peaceful life, and his attachment to his family:

> 'Tis but too true that I have not the means to live there as I have for years been accustomed to. On my own Account I care little but am attached to my family and should have wished to provide more substantially for them. However, they are all Predestinarians and will attribute the loss, not to my fault, but their own Stars.
> . . . At Khasgunge I anticipate very great happiness. I delight in having nothing to do, I am fond of reading and am fond of my Garden and (there's no accounting for tastes) have more relish in playing with the little Brats than for the first Society in the World. The Begum and I, in 22 years constant contact, have smoothed off each other's asperities and roll on peaceably and contentedly. (5 March 1820)

Gardner's concern with making adequate provision for his family dominates his letters to Edward Gardner. He is obviously very fond of his children and grandchildren and says quite explicitly here that he would rather spend time with them than with "the first Society in the World." His relationship with his wife is elsewhere portrayed in the language of a humorously querulous old man. When he doesn't hear from his family, he gets anxious: "I believe the folks at Khassgunge are all Baked or Bedevilled, I have not had a line these 12 days, and some of them used to write to me daily" (Letter 80, Babel 24 June 1821). From his letters, it becomes clear that the separation of Gardner from his family is a hardship for his wife as well. Using his usual combination of raillery and wit, he writes that she has urged him to "leave the service and come starve at Khassgunge" (Letter 80, 24 June 1821). The Begum had made some financial calculations to persuade Gardner that they would have enough to live on, but Gardner thinks it involves counting on certain eventualities such as fixed taxes and price of grain to feed his horses that were not that certain. This exchange reveals the close relationship that Gardner had with his wife and extended family and the good humor with which they seem to have maintained it. When Gardner died in 1835, Fanny Parkes wrote:

> My beloved friend Colonel Gardner . . . was buried, according to his desire, near the [domed Mughal] tomb of his son Allan. From the time of his death the poor Begum pined and sank daily; just as he said she complained not, but she took his death to heart; she died one month and two days after his decease. (Parkes 458)

The romance of Gardner and his wife thus had a long life and was carried through even into death, surely a historical instance of a happy interracial marriage such as we do not find in literary texts later in the century. Late-nineteenth- and early-twentieth-century literary texts fail to imagine this kind of domestic life and shy away from representing mixed-race children.

The narrative I have reconstructed reveals the unacknowledged cultural mixing in an interracial household and the indigenization of Englishmen, owed in large part to their Indian partners. The women, even in a segregated Muslim society, enjoyed social and political power and built alliances with other powerful families. In this episode, the romance of empire is about the unexpected sharing of domestic power between an English man and a Muslim woman and their exploration of a syncretic lifestyle; it thus presents a critique of the idea of British benevolence as the core of the romance of Anglo-Indian life. As a coda to this romance, and further evidence of the direction of cultural syncretism, it is worth noting that one of Gardner's grandsons adopted the traditions of Mughal courtly culture of the mid-eighteenth century and became a noted poet in Urdu. The fact that nine members of the family took on Urdu pen names and became prolific poets have led scholars to note that "there is probably no other Anglo-Indian family of India which has produced so many poets of Urdu" (Saksena 101). Suleiman Shikoh, Gardner's grandson, is reported to have been fluent in Arabic, Persian, English, Urdu, Hindi, and had, in addition, a smattering of Pashto. He achieved some literary fame with his writings in Persian, Hindi, and Urdu. He was also considered to be a patron of poets and a famous poet, Jan Sahab, after many wanderings, was given refuge by Suleiman Shikoh and ultimately died there. His son, Daniel Nathaniel Gardner, also named "Shukr" studied with the scholar Mirza Abbas Hussain Hosh Lucknavi. He went on to write poetry in Urdu and Persian, though the complete collection of his poems is untraced. He contributed to literary magazines, especially *Guldastai* in the period 1885–1886 (Saksena 120–21). I recount this narrative of Gardner's grandson and great-grandson to show how for Gardner's family a kind of absorption into Muslim culture happened steadily through the next three generations and after. If the romance of empire is about educating good citizens of empire and turning them into quasi-colonials, this narrative moves the other way, absorbing the Englishman ultimately into the traditions of the land that he made his home.

CHAPTER TWO

The Home and the Bazaar
The Anglo-Indian Novels of Bithia Mary Croker

In the early twentieth century, interracial marriages and mixed homes appear frequently in writing by women romancers. They explore the permutations of nineteenth-century domestic ideology abroad, and have, until fairly recently, been an unexplored resource for understanding colonial culture.[1] In fact, in 1972, Benita Parry made the following comments about Anglo-Indian romancers: "while they deal in superficialities and received opinions, their fiction innocently reveals the sensations which India could evoke in impressionable British people. The themes they repeatedly use point to the way Anglo-Indians were haunted by Indian sensuality and spirituality" (Parry 70). I show how these romances make a significant contribution to literary history by challenging the conventions of the Victorian domestic novel and by making the non-European woman insistently part of 'English' life abroad. The traditional closure of the domestic and adventure novel[2] and its elimination of racial difference are challenged by the appearance of interracial domesticity in these romances.[3]

Given the predominance of the masculine genre of the 'adventure' novel as the representative literature of empire, it comes as something of a surprise that in the early part of the twentieth century, Anglo-Indian women writers such as Alice Perrin, Maud Diver, I. A. R. Wylie, Fanny Penny, and Bithia Mary Croker were very popular, often commanding very large audiences all over the world. This body of fiction represents Victorian experience abroad, and exposes and explores Victorian ideologies of gender, nation, and class when recreated in the colonies. Nancy Paxton offers one explanation for the proliferation of romances after 1857, arguing that "female" romances describing interracial marriage became possible because the new "racialization of difference acted to eroticize Indian women and men in new ways, thus undermining the dominant rape script of the postmutiny period" (Paxton, "Secrets" 193).[4] The romances of Bithia Mary Croker are a particularly rich and provocative example of this genre, enacting both the fascination and the fear of hybrid domestic spaces. I explore the representation of miscegenation and interracial marriage in two of Croker's Indian romances, *The Company's Servant* (1908) and *In Old Madras* (1913), focusing mainly on the latter.[5]

In most Victorian novels, the motif of the return to England has meant that miscegenation is their repressed and rejected narrative.[6] Literary antecedents for the interracial marriage between a British man and a native woman can be found in Kipling's early tales, Conrad's Malay tales and *Lord Jim*, and Robert Louis Stevenson's *The Beach of Falesa*. But in these works, it is depicted either in the register of the dreamlike, unreal, and exotic, or as a repressed and unspeakable transgression. One of Kipling's early stories, "Beyond the Pale," might stand as a literary precursor to Croker's *In Old Madras*. The interracial love between the English hero and a young Indian widow is punished in the end by the gruesome mutilation of the woman and the banishment of her English lover from the Indian spaces in which he had become comfortable. He is wounded in his right leg and returns to his English world with that as a reminder of his transgression. The aberration is covered over and his respectability is reestablished with the return to England. In Croker's Anglo-Indian romances, on the other hand, interracial romances are represented as an unavoidable part of the terrain, and given fuller treatment.

Reading popular literature as a rich source for the social and cultural life of a period is a well-established strategy in literary and even historical studies. In colonial India, romances read in conjunction with 'official' sources enable us to analyze those pockets of silence in canonical texts that circumscribe a further and fuller investigation of topics such as miscegenation and interracial romance. Popular forms of writing and representation often express unacknowledged fears, anxieties, and preoccupations by associating in new and original ways different genres of writing. The potential of the popular to open up all kinds of subversive patterns of readerly identification has been the subject of much debate in studies of Victorian popular texts. In such discussions, reading is conceived of as an active process which can refuse or transform a text. As Liggins and Duffy write, "popular writers were constantly engaged in subverting expectations about genre while remaining within the broad confines of generic conventions, which helped to give readers more scope for interpretation" (Liggins and Duffy xix). This scholarship provides a useful point of comparison for strategies of reading colonial texts which neither conclusively break away from Victorian ideologies and narrative forms, nor simply mimic them. In my study of the Anglo-Indian romance, therefore, I have focused on unraveling the complex patterns of identification and rejection in the familiar form of the domestic novel that create the texture of its representation of natives, others, and cultural difference.

I. "Astonishingly workmanlike and readable"

Anglo-Indian romances, also called "Indian Romance" (Stieg 2) or "Anglo-Indian domestic novels" (Sainsbury 163), were produced between 1880 and 1930 and were immensely popular with British women readers in India, England, and in British colonies.[7] An early study by Bhupal Singh recognizes the romances as a distinctive genre and classifies them by plot and theme.[8] Within this genre, interracial romances (usually between an English man and an Indian woman) constitute another subgenre and more often than not end with the death of the Indian woman. Maud Diver is one of the few authors whose three interracial romances, *Lilamani* (1909), *Far to Seek: A Romance of England and India* (1921), and *The Dream Prevails* (1938), have happy endings. At the other end of the spectrum, the theme of Pamela Wynne's romances, which often narrate the sad fate of English women who fall prey to Indian men, is best described by their titles: *East Is Always East* (1930) and *Ann's an Idiot* (1923). A more typical plot follows the fortunes of an English man or woman of the upper or middle class who travels to India, develops a love for the country, finds an English love-interest of the appropriate class, and returns to England to establish happy domesticity. Often, one of the protagonists falls on hard times and has to struggle to find a place in the upper-middle class society of Anglo-Indians, where he or she is finally restored to a place of honor by inheriting a fortune or a title. Sometimes, as in Alice Perrin's *The Anglo-Indians* (1913), the love for India and the fantasy of a pastoral, feudal lifestyle take the happy couple back to India. Fictional examples of liaisons between English men and Indian women, which invariably end with the death of the woman, make it apparent that such a connection between the two worlds has no narrative or social viability. In Flora Annie Steel's *On the Face of the Waters* (1896), the young Indian mistress of the English hero fades away into a pale wraith, by her death releasing the hero to marry an English woman. Similarly, the Indian wife of a British official in Philip Meadows Taylor's *Seeta* (1872) dies in the Revolt of 1857, thereby resolving the problem of finding credible social possibilities for her within Anglo-India. The unofficial status of interracial romance gives it a tragic, Gothic, and subterranean life in the imagination of the Anglo-Indian romancers.

Early-twentieth-century women romancers have not received the same serious critical attention as canonical figures such as Rudyard Kipling and E. M. Forster, who have always been studied for the seriousness and complexity of their Indian experience. Domestic dramas and romances have been treated as at best a historical curiosity and at worst "bad writing" that would never attain the status of great literature. So it is not surprising that very little is known about Croker except that she was the daughter of an Irish clergyman and married a John Croker who rose to be Lieutenant-Colonel in the Royal Munster Fusiliers posted in India. Even though she wrote fifty novels (twenty of which set in India), she receives only brief mention in dictionaries of Irish writers and *The Feminist Companion to Literature in English*. The *Feminist Companion* tells us that Croker spent fourteen years in Burma and India, where in 1880 she began writing as a distraction from the hot season (248)! Croker published some of her fiction in *Cornhill Magazine* and *Belgravia*. Her first novel, *Proper Pride,* had good reviews but was thought to be by a man.

Responses to Croker's fiction in the contemporary press ranged from enthusiastic appreciation to faintly derogatory comments about the lack of depth in her characters or worse, her bad punctuation. A satirical and irreverent obituary article in *The Bookman* in January 1921 begins with the unpromising statement that Mrs. Croker "will be missed as a woman, even more than as an author" (Pure 311). Croker, the reviewer says, had "two strings to her bow," Ireland and India, the first acquired by birth and the second by long residence in India, but "if the patterns she worked with were largely the same," that would not "displease her patron in the least" (Pure 311). One of her early novels, *Beyond the Pale,* is described as "astonishingly workmanlike and readable." This shaky edifice of approval is completely destroyed, however, by the remark that Mrs. Croker used the comma to "devastate perfectly clear English"

(Pure 312). But if these reviews did not add greatly to Croker's reputation as a novelist, other journals did take favorable notice. *The Times Literary Supplement* in a 1902 book review described *The Cat's Paw* as having "abundance of sensation, with unwonted freshness of incident," while *In Old Madras* "shows [Croker's] usual ease and familiarity in picturing Anglo-Indian life" (44). By the end of the century, Croker had reason to feel pleased with her success as a popular author. She wrote to a friend in May 1895: "I get up to 100 pounds for barely 30,000 words now, cash down, and I have promised the back reprints of three novels; so you see I am getting on at last, and time for me, seeing that I have brought out *eleven* successful books in twelve years—not that any of them were boomed or made a great splash—but they secured the attention of plenty of readers in England, America, Australia, Germany, and side stations"[9] (emphasis in original).

We can conclude that there was a large market for Croker's fiction from the fact that many of her novels were published by Tauchnitz, one of the largest European publishing houses. Founded by Baron Tauchnitz, this house was one of the leading publishers of English language fiction in the nineteenth century.[10] It was also well known for producing cheap editions of the work of some of the most prominent Victorian novelists such as George Eliot, Anthony Trollope, and Wilkie Collins. The Tauchnitz edition of *In Old Madras* includes on its front and back cover advertisements for other fiction by very popular writers including H. Rider Haggard's *Child of Storm*, Jack London's *South Sea Tales*, and *The Mating of Lydia* by Mrs. Humphrey Ward. The continental publication of this edition shows that Croker's novels had a large audience that extended beyond their obvious constituencies in England and India.[11] Baron Tauchnitz organized a vast distribution system in Europe, where his books were sold in public places like railways stations, stores, and stalls. Tauchnitz books could also be found in the libraries of resort hotels and ships at sea, and "at such remote locales as Algiers, Luxor, Meknes, and Port Sudan, at Buenos Aires, Montvideo, Rio de Janeiro, and Santiago, and at Kobe, Peking, Smyrna, and Teheran" (Todd and Bowden 190).

The expatriate British in India, as they appear in these romances, constitute a small insular community and think of the 'mysterious East' and 'native character' in fairly stereotypical ways. Englishness is imagined as enclosed towns and houses with neat ordered gardens and cool, well-decorated interiors. In this spatial scheme, Indian spaces such as the jungle and the bazaar are disordered and threatening, although the romances also celebrate the beauty of the hills, valleys, and lush vegetation. As Allan Greenberger points out, the depiction of India in the romances was largely confined to the frontier, rural areas, jungles or small hill-stations but especially in the novels of Kipling and Croker, "the geographic area itself is looked upon as possessing certain characteristics" (Greenberger 40). The romantic and picturesque depictions of the Indian landscape are posited on a separation of the races and are interrupted by the presence of the Eurasian characters (Greenberger 70).

Set against an exotic backdrop, Anglo-Indian fiction portrays interracial romance either as another thrilling adventure that comes to an end with the convenient death of the native woman, or as a Gothic aberration and an instance of the perils of stepping out of the boundaries of the British and the familiar. As Greenberger's comment implies, the death of the Indian wife or mistress has been read as a reflection of contemporary social reality. But this view assumes that the imaginative reach of fiction is circumscribed by the available social horizon that it must represent, and that it was the peculiar character of Anglo-Indian fiction to represent official ideology. Such a conception of the formal and historical determinants of Anglo-Indian fiction does not account for the buried, the marginal, the forbidden social phenomena that Croker's fiction represents. In her novels, normative English domestic values are precarious and beleaguered and the departures from official ideology are as compelling as the pleasures of bourgeois domesticity.

Popular fiction is often read as a transparent reproduction of official ideology and the popular appeal of Anglo-Indian romances did lie in the repetition of certain plots, themes, narrative patterns, stereotypes, each focused on heterosexual romance and the 'happy ending' that confirmed imperial power. But as I argue, this seemingly simple movement of the plot is countered by the persistent focus on interracial marriage and its pervasive presence in the romances. Anglo-Indian romances enacted a fantasy of upward mobility in their plot, and, as in other moments of history, created a readership for which a protected domestic sphere constituted the success of Empire.

The efficient management of a European home acquired great significance in the colonies, as Ann Stoler tells us, because it ensured that the men would be protected from contact with native women, and avoiding racial degeneracy would strengthen their imperial ambitions.[12] Stoler's larger point in her study is that the "arrival in large numbers of European women thus coincided with an embourgeoisment of colonial communities and with a significant sharpening of racial categories" (Stoler 1991 64). Furthermore, these racial distinctions were expressed in the language of class, which in turn underscored colonial authority.

Stoler also points out that in making domestic arrangements between Dutch colonials and Asian women, the Dutch recognized that at stake were critical issues such as the power that native women might exercise over Company officials and how this might affect administration. The progeny of mixed marriages had to be provided for, often through the channels of official employment. If they were to be abandoned, then personal and official duty could clash, thus leading to a disruption of the functioning of colonial rule (Stoler 1990).

The British seemed rather more squeamish than French or Dutch colonials about recognizing liaisons with native women. Given this scenario, and her status as a writer of popular fiction, the foregrounding of interracial marriage and hybrid households in Bithia Mary Croker's *In Old Madras* is startling and deserving of critical attention. While other Anglo-Indian romance writers also venture into this terrain, Croker's fiction dwells on transgression and miscegenation with horrified fascination. Her interest, though, is not in celebrating this hybrid domestic space, but in expressing the anxiety that English women's social options shrink alarmingly when India as a marriage market disappoints their expectations. Many of the women in Croker's novels, destitute and without alternative social options, represent the large population of educated, middle-class, socially superfluous single women in England who left for foreign parts to seek their fortune. India thus becomes both a place of exotic fantasy where domestic ambition and romantic aspiration are realized, but also a place where Eurasian and Indian women can usurp the place of the domestic angel in the English home.

The popularity of Croker's romances compels us to question the nature of readerly pleasure in the text. Romances that focus on miscegenation complicate our notion of simple escape, which is now figured as the vicarious transgression of racial boundaries. Did these romances work to consolidate middle-class ideologies that created good wives at home, or did they offer a secret frisson of delight in what lay outside the home? How are English weddings that signal the formal closures of the romance offset by the forbidden pleasures of miscegenation? I will return to these questions to determine the significance of Anglo-Indian romances in the literature of empire.

II. In Old Madras

In Old Madras is set up as a pseudo-suspense novel with an unresolved mystery providing the motive for the action. The young English hero

Geoffrey Mallendar comes to India in search of his uncle, Captain Mallendar, who has been missing for many years and has been given up for dead. Geoffrey's suspicions are aroused by the fact that someone draws on his uncle's bank account regularly, and against the injunctions of his uncle's business partners and the advice of friends and family, he decides to investigate this mystery. He is duly introduced into Anglo-Indian society and meets a diverse cast of characters: the married Tallboys happily ensconced in upper-class domesticity; the miserable single women Barbie Miller and Ada Sims, seeking husbands or patrons; the ruthless and extravagant widow Lena Villars, also seeking a husband; the malicious gossip Mrs. Fiske; and the friendly, unpretentious cousin Nancy Brander. Geoffrey falls in love with Barbie Miller and after many adventures that take him to the margins of Anglo-Indian society, earns the title to his father's estate, marries Barbie, and returns triumphant to England. The climactic episode is the discovery of his uncle, the missing Captain Mallendar. Unlike most other romances in this genre, *In Old Madras* does not dwell on the central love plot between Geoffrey and Barbie, which is given fairly perfunctory treatment. Croker's imaginative energies are spent in taking Geoffrey and the reader through a tour of the peripheries of Anglo-Indian society, into interracial homes and mixed domestic spaces, and finally to the confrontation with Geoffrey's uncle. It is only then that the sentimental plot concludes with the wedding of Barbie and Geoffrey. Croker's preoccupation with interracial relationships in this romance makes the English domesticity of the Tallboys a normative referent, not the center of the action.

We are introduced to this English ideal of domesticity early in the novel in the person of Fanny Tallboys, the perfect hostess, homemaker, and therefore perfect wife of Fred Tallboys, Geoffrey Mallendar's cousin. Her parties are the most successful and well attended in her circle, and her house is always full of well looked-after guests. At his first dinner in her house, Mallendar and the company are:

> ... steered successfully into their respective places at an oval table, glittering with crystal and silver and embellished by exquisite flowers and fruit. In the background stood a row of well-drilled attendants, commanded and marshalled by the gold and white butler.... The new-comer noted the dainty appointments and careful details, painted menus, crested Venetian glass, and three superb epergnes.... (54)

As one of the guests says to Mallendar, "we're quite up to date here" (54), pointing to the successful duplication of English upper-class society by Anglo-Indians. Further evidence of Mrs. Tallboys's skill as a hostess is provided when Mallendar learns that one of her passions is acquiring antique furniture. This is almost the first thing he notices in her living room, which characterizes her in his mind even before he meets her:

> He did not fail to notice the great chunam pillars—gleaming like white marble—the polished teak floors, Eastern rugs, carefully placed screens, and profusion of delicately scented flowers; the whole atmosphere exhaled a cultivated taste, and subdued magnificence. What particularly struck the stranger was the accumulation of old furniture; objects he recognized from seeing their counterparts in great houses—or indeed in a lesser degree his own. Here were chairs, mirrors, settees, and cabinets—enclosing curiosities and old china. Mallender was no judge, but he realized that he was surrounded by many rare and valuable treasures. . . . (50)

The Tallboyses' residence is a reminder of the British aspirations to an aristocratic lifestyle that India permitted without the privilege of noble birth. Fanny Tallboys does not come from a titled family, though Fred Tallboys certainly belongs to the landed gentry. The political dominance of the British, the comforts provided by a high-paying official position, and servants in the household allowed the upper echelons of the bureaucracy to not only imitate, but recreate on an even grander scale, the lifestyle of titled and landed gentry in England. Describing Hoopers Gardens, the Tallboys' residence in Madras, Byng explains to Geoffrey that the great houses here are "not like our Grosvenor Gardens or Chesterfield Gardens, at home; these houses—sort of nabob's palaces—built by merchants in the Fort, were where they took refuge during the longshore winds . . . " (31). The extravagance of the Tallboys' lifestyle is tempered by the fact that they generously share their home with others and that Mrs. Tallboys is active in charitable work—the mark of Victorian upper- and middle-class women.

The markers of the Tallboyses' aristocratic status such as "rare and valuable treasures" can be easily acquired in India without necessarily inheriting them through the family. This is made evident in Fanny Tallboys's description of the process by which she acquired her furniture "in the thieving bazaar, or at Franck's auction rooms in Mount Road" (52):

> That lovely Empire Couch he [Fred] rescued from being chopped up for firewood—the poor thing had only two legs. The Chippendale chairs he routed out of a mouldy old bungalow on the top of Palaveram Hill. I

discovered that charming satinwood table, in a dirzee's shop of Blacktown; some of the furniture has made journeys all over the Presidency on bullock-carts when regiments were on the move, and has been battered and cracked and auctioned, over and over again, for nearly two centuries!

... some invaluable treasures have gone to boil cooltie, or gram, but many fine seasoned travelers still survive. My collection is my craze, my chief weakness, and my tongue once started cannot stop; every bit has its own history. Those Sevres vases I bought from a Toda in the Hills; that ugly gilt jar in the same cabinet, I purchased as an act of charity from a beggar, a poor Eurasian woman, and gave her twenty rupees—believing it was brass. Long afterwards it turned out to be solid gold—a bit of loot from Seringapatam. (52)

Fanny's list of salvaged furniture shows how the features of an Anglo-Indian home have meaning only when they are assembled and arranged according to the conventions of a bourgeois home. Wrenched from that context, unappreciated, and gathering dust in the shops and houses of Indians, they signify nothing except the failure of cultural transposition and a history of plunder. Significantly, the vase that the Eurasian woman sells is part of the plunder from Seringapatam, sacked by the British in 1799. As relics of a bygone era, they do not impinge on the lives of the natives, which go on regardless of the detritus of past historical moments. When Fanny Tallboys refers to every piece having its own history, she means the history it has acquired when collected by Fanny. The Eurasian woman, dislocated and unmoored from a stable social context as a consequence of mixed blood, does not even know whether she is selling gold or brass. These objects, native and European alike, acquire semiotic significance only when they are arranged in Fanny Tallboys's living room. They also evoke the time of individual adventurers and profiteers who came to India often in the service of the East India Company, but also as agents of traders or with independent commissions in the army in the second half of the eighteenth century. This was the period that created the nabob whose wealth acquired mythic status in England and India.

In Old Madras provides several studies in dramatic contrasts. If the happy and luxurious life of the Tallboyses is one end of the spectrum, Croker does not mince her words when representing the extreme economic destitution of lower-middle-class women at the other end who appear on the margins of the social world of *In Old Madras*. The dream of happy matrimony against an exotic backdrop fails more often than it succeeds and exposes the underside of the fantasy of India as a marriage market for Englishwomen. For many of the women, India fails to fulfill the dream of happy matrimony and upward social mobility against an exotic backdrop. Ada Sim is a grim reminder of the lack of social options for such women in the late nineteenth century. She is introduced to Mallendar at a grand dinner at his cousin Major Tallboys's house as "a dreadful sponge and not very interesting" (57) by the dazzling Mrs. Villars, a rich widow searching for a second husband. Ada's friend Barbie Miller, who eventually becomes the hero's love interest, is also placed in a similar position and is threatened with the prospect of marrying a wealthy bachelor almost twice her age. As the two women exchange confidences, Ada Sim reveals that she has exhausted all her resources and the goodwill of her friends. She cannot pay for her passage back to England, and has been reduced to selling her clothes. Even the possibility of ending it all is denied the wretched Ada as she says with a touch of black humor: "I'd drown myself, only there is no place to do it in—the Cooum is filthy, and off the pier there are sharks" (73). In the depth of her self-hating despair, she points out to Barbie why she cannot find a niche in Anglo-Indian society: "Friends, I have none, those I had are sick of me, and no wonder. I'm not pretty, or amusing, or accomplished, I don't play bridge for money, I'm not even good-tempered. Just a plain, stupid bore" (73).

Ada is the anti-heroine who is unable to participate in the endless rounds of dinners, bridge playing, singing, dancing, and flirting that characterize Anglo-Indian society. From the account that she gives of her life in England, we learn that she was an orphan who lived with her aunt as maid and governess to her two children. To escape the drudgery of her life, she "devoured every book relating to the East" that she could find. Her sister's letters from India make it a place of escape, adventure, and romance. Once in India, Ada finds the reality quite different from the romance. Relying on her ability to sing, tell fortunes, and trim hats, Ada enjoys her first few months in India, being "reckless, and happy, and greedy of amusement" (119). As she goes from one friend's house to the next, she finds herself less and less welcome and slowly turns into an unwanted guest. Her aunt, who thinks Ada had been reckless and unwise, "wild-goosing to India" (118), refuses to help her out of her dire financial distress.

The story of Ada Sim shows that the Anglo-Indian social world, which mostly works as a marriage market, enforces quite rigorously a certain economy of desire. Ada comes to a sad pass because she travels to India, not primarily with the aim of finding a husband, and thereby establishing stable domesticity, but to have "a ripping time" (118). Added to this situation is the prejudice of Anglo-Indian society which has no place for a single working woman without the privilege of wealth and class. Ada's ability to provide for herself and the fact that she does not seem to be actively soliciting a husband, makes her social position indeterminate.

This policing of women's desires takes a similar form in Croker's treatment of the harsh, uncharitable, but glamorous Mrs. Villars. The author's unsparing scrutiny of Mrs. Villars makes it quite clear that she is as much of a sponge, to use her own words, as Ada Sim. Unlike Ada, she is looking for a husband who will provide her with the extravagant lifestyle to which she is accustomed. In the moral economy of the novel, Lena Villars comes off worse than anybody else. In trying to be a siren to Mallendar, she is only following instructions from Fanny, who has been asked by her husband to distract Mallendar from his crazy quest for his uncle. But when she decides to woo him with the intention of marrying him, the narrative voice exults over her failure to trap the hero. The harsh judgment of the narrative voice is turned on her only when she begins to play in earnest the part that she is expected to play only in jest. Lena Villars is judged for sins of economic profligacy and moral irresponsibility, both of which are threatening to the Anglo-Indian domestic sphere.

The wish-fulfilling function of the Anglo-Indian romance pushes the plot to a happy conclusion for its economically dispossessed women. But this is only achieved through the intercession of patriarchal figures. Fanny Tallboys finds Major Tallboys, while Ada Sim is rescued by a friend of her uncle who intercedes with him on her behalf. The uncle, ending a long-standing estrangement, turns into her benefactor and gives her a place in his home. Barbie is 'rescued' from marrying a much older man by Mallendar, the heir to the Mallendar estate. The formal movement of the romance reestablishes domestic harmony and benevolent kinship relations and India remains a wish-fulfilling land, a place where destitute Englishwomen are rescued and securely placed in the English household.

If a happy ending were all that *In Old Madras* concerned itself with, it would not distinguish itself in the huge corpus of Anglo-Indian romances. But the romance takes us on a journey away from Anglo-India towards racially mixed domestic spaces and the secret, obscure, or entirely absent social lives of Englishmen who are detached or estranged from the hub of Anglo-India. Their miscegenated relationships are expressed in a vision of Gothic disorder inside the house. If the romance has earlier been haunted by the possibility of racial contamination, it now boldly goes forth into these racially mixed areas. Furthermore, the rescue motif works now in relation to Englishmen who are saved and provided nurture by women of Indian or Eurasian origin or of the lower class.

In their instructions for household management, Maud Diver and Flora Annie Steel describe the English household as similar to the 'Indian Empire' in its organization and management. There is no opposition between the nature and character of the household and the empire, but in fact they exist in the same continuum. Croker's fiction also establishes the importance of the English household to an articulation of English values, but in an important difference from Diver, Steel, and Gardiner, in her fiction the Indian spaces outside the household are not brought under the purview of British governance. The jungle and the bazaar, in particular, are represented as 'Indian' spaces which fill the Anglo-Indian viewer with fear and bewilderment. The protective and nurturing influence of the English household is thus countered by the risk to British men from the India that cannot be understood in the terms of Anglo-India. Croker's fictional and ideological terrain is thus mapped onto a geography of spaces. The most extreme form of racial and cultural panic occurs when Indian values and sociality invade the English household in the form of Indian wives and mixed children, thereby transforming the domestic space as well.

Croker's fiction invokes the genre of Gothic fiction in its focus on dramatic eruptions, threatening exotic spaces, taboo themes such as miscegenation, and disordered interiors of homes. It shares with other examples of the genre a bourgeois fear of the cultural other. In an important study of the Gothic, Kate Ellis defines it as "a set of conventions to represent what is not supposed to exist" (7). These conventions are expressed as an intrusion of the spectral or the monstrous into the domestic and sentimental family plot, which is usually eliminated at the end. In the romances, the Gothic makes visible that which realistic or sentimental fiction would repress or erase; for example, miscegenation, a subject actively resisted by the Victorian novel.

In Croker's fiction, the Gothic originates not only in easily available stereotypes of the racial other, but also in the Englishwoman's anxiety about the usurpation of the English domestic space by Indian women. The language of domestic realism mixes with the monstrous forms of hybrid households to produce a new kind of racial Gothic. Yet, as I show, in Croker's fiction, while the miscegenated households are rejected on the one hand, they are also domesticated and become places of nurture and sociability.[13] They do not disappear at the conclusion of the narrative, and even though the narrative effect Croker wants to achieve is horror at the hybrid households of interracial families, this horror is tempered by the survival of these households in defiance of Anglo-Indian norms. Despite the narrative return to England, and Croker's anxiety about maintaining an English household, her fiction dwells on miscegenated households with a desiring glance that contradicts narrative outcome. Not only are the Indian and/or lower-class women granted representational space in Croker's romances, they are often the primary caretakers of the English men they marry. Often, a trace of the Indian experience travels back to England, as in the case of the Indian-born golden-haired girls who return to England in triumph with their English foster parents. This return to England suggests the overriding importance of the production and articulation of class in gendered terms in the construction of imperial culture, a subject to which I shall return in my discussion of miscegenated domesticity.

When the young Mallendar goes in search of his uncle, he is provided with many false clues that lead him to other British men who live with Indian or lower class wives and have produced "half-caste" children, and who, as a consequence, are hiding from Anglo-India in the obscure life of some small town. The first of these false leads takes Mallendar to the home of Major Rochfort, who has a wife in England and a second family with a half-Indian wife on a plantation in India. The Major's second wife has passed away and his household now includes their three children, a daughter "who looks quite Europe" and two sons who, though the image of their father, are "two copies in black" (164). The fair color and golden hair of the girl, Mota, who is beautiful, whimsical and sometimes wayward, extracts tribute from siblings and friends alike, expressing her sense of her racial and cultural superiority.

The climax of this episode comes when the Major's first wife visits India and discovers his second family. She finds that his second wife, though only half-European, is a beautiful and graceful woman who has kept a lovely home. This fact gives her the narrator's approval, and unlike other greedy, grasping "Delilah" figures who try to lure British officers into matrimony, she is portrayed as having had a positive effect on the Major's life. Even Mallendar, who has seen the Major's English and Indian homes, recognizes this:

> Then, he had sat at a table loaded with wonderful old silver and hot-house flowers, and was waited on by powdered footmen, in the company of Rochfort's prim English wife, and her titled county neighbours.

> Now, he was eating curried vegetables, under a slowly moving punkah, attended by black servants, and surrounded by a Madras family—which included a golden-haired imperious hostess, aged nine years. (184)

As Major Rochfort's first wife takes in the details of the Madras home, she perceives an implied criticism of her domestic life in England. She notices "the homely comfort, the good plain food . . . the bright young people, and their complete absence of self-consciousness" (184). Impressed with this picture of the happy family in a well-appointed home, and the charming Mota, Mrs. Rochfort decides to adopt Mota, make peace with her husband, and return to England. India provides yet another happy resolution as the Major's empty domestic life in England is enriched by love and affection for the young girl. The golden-haired child redeems the racially mixed households by offering the possibility of assimilation back into British culture. Mota can travel to England and become part of British family because she can pass as white. In its 'happy' dénouements, the romance tries to erase traces of the Indian experience and return to pristine English domesticity. The young English girl is a visible symbol of this possibility, though it is significant that she has Indian blood and was raised in India.

A slightly older version of Mota appears in the next episode in the household of General Beamish, a retired army officer who is found in the small town of Wellunga by Mallendar as he continues the search for his uncle. This time, she is called Tara, an adopted child of the General and his wife and described as belonging to "a totally different type and race, evidently a 'throw-back' to some of the General's ancestors" (215). Clearly she does not belong to Mrs. Beamish, who is introduced to Mallendar by the General as "my third wife, country born, country bred, no country blood though—just an apothecary's daughter, and a trained nurse; but I did not marry her for that" (211). Although Mrs. Beamish is probably white, she is clearly of a lower class than the General. Croker's representation of her and her children is startlingly similar to her depiction of Eurasian characters—the language of class and race work interchangeably in this fictional universe.

This is transparently evident in Croker's idiom of domestic interiors which mark racial and class difference through their difference from an ideal of pure English culture. General Beamish's house is described as a "mixture" in much the same way as the inhabitants:

> In fact, the appointments and surroundings were a curious and remarkable mixture; here were rat-tailed spoons, Charles the First Sugar bowls,

superb candelabra, holding cheap candles (twelve to the pound), a coarse mission table-cloth, and bazaar crockery. The aristocratic sideboard, and a bookcase were undoubtedly of the days of Count Lally, and seemed to shrivel up, and hold themselves aloof from the coarse "maistrey" furniture and jail carpets—their associates. (215)

The mismatched interiors reflect a crossing of class boundaries and a falling off from the glamour and harmony of Anglo-India. The company is also "strangely assorted" (215)—Mrs. Beamish and her children Jessie and Tom are described as "a kindly commonplace trio, of the lower middle class," while the two daughters of a family friend look only half-European. The racial features of General Beamish's children by a woman of the lower classes are juxtaposed with the "maistry" furniture (furniture made by a local Indian carpenter) and the mismatched china. The interior of the home also acquires the marks of race and class as a reflection of those who constitute the household. It would be difficult to ignore Croker's racial and racist depiction of the binaries of English and other, but the much-maligned household is a home nevertheless, not a fantastic space that threatens to dissolve with narrative closure as in the case of so many adventure novels. Croker interrupts the progress of exotic adventure and romance with mundane and detailed descriptions of the household. The superb candelabra hold candles that cost twelve to the pound, indicating the contribution of Mrs. Beamish to the household in contrast to the upper-class origins of the General. Significantly, Mrs. Beamish was a trained nurse, and although the General self-consciously claims that he did not marry her for that, she is clearly the manager and caretaker of the home.

Croker's revulsion from the mixed household at first suggests both her racist and class-centered view of cultural hybridity, and in fact, one is constitutive of the other. Yet her ambivalence towards an aristocratic extravagance and towards the high European culture, marked by French-influenced cuisine, and the latest gowns and dresses that arrive from the continent, are also evident everywhere. Croker's middle-class gaze satirically cuts down the snobbish and malicious Mrs. Fiske, who would never associate with natives or with people whose wealth and social standing were not apparent. The middle-class virtues of economy and good home management are much valued in this Anglo-Indian world. As Mallendar's lively, affectionate cousin, Mrs. Nancy Brander points out, "it is a good thing to encourage your cook, put him on his mettle and, so to speak, *lard* him with flattery" (62). The European treasures in the great house are admired to the detriment of native craftsmen, who can clearly only produce poor imitations of European furniture or European dresses. But while Croker sneers at Mrs. Beamish's "maistry" (carpenter) furniture, she also castigates extravagance that amounts to pretension. At Fanny Tallboys's party, Lena Villers, the high priestess of fashion, compliments Nancy Brander on the "French effect" (68) of her dress and is shocked to discover that it was made by a *dirzee* [an Indian tailor]. Nancy retorts that she cut it with her own hands, "and my man is an artist" (69) defending her *dirzee* and her economical use of money and resources. The sympathetic representation of the sensible Mrs. Brander is a foil for the extravagant and self-indulgent Lena, who is punished for her profligacy when she is forced to dupe an older man to marry her and clear her of her debts.

Similarly, Mrs. Beamish, if not quite up to the upper-class lifestyle of the Tallboyses, and "country-born" and "country-bred," is nevertheless given the respect due to a nurse and pharmacist. Mallendar is astonished to find a large crowd outside the Beamish residence one day, " a multitude of the blind, halt, and lame, all waiting to be treated by the kind hands of Mrs. Beamish" (241). And as Mrs. Beamish, justifiably proud of her clientele says, "Look at my clients—has any doctor in Harley Street such a practice" (242)! [sic].

If the cultural intermixing within households evokes an ambivalent response in Croker, the Indian bazaar seems an even more confused, disordered, unenclosed space that resists British classification. It is a place where people jostle and crowd together in a close interaction with "the low-Other . . . hybrid, heterogeneous, and ambiguous . . . Bourgeois society construes as contamination the mixing of classes and other social and cultural categories that is essential to the marketplace or fair."[14] Croker's Indian bazaar is represented as a place of congenial, if bewildering, abundance:

> In the first place, although it was teeming with human life, there was not a single European to be seen, nor even a Eurasian—all were natives of the country. Truly here was "India for the Indians!" The stalls displayed no Western requirements, but grains, condiments, strange sweets, coloured cottons, and muslins, piles of silk of local manufacture in vermilion, orange, indigo, pink and green; also turbans, and tinseled caps of all colours. Here were working jewellers with their little braziers; huka makers, weavers of spells, and public letter-writers. The long narrow streets reeked with the intangible but familiar bazaar odour (a mixture of oil, grain, aromatic spices, and raw cotton). Crowds were chafing, gossiping, or strolling along. Here and there, a tall bold-

looking woman covered with jewellery, and painted with kohl, passed with defiant glare; gaily caparisoned horses with jewelled girths, and head-bands—their manes and tails dyed rose colour—were led snorting by disturbing the little sacred bulls, who were poking wet black noses into the open gram baskets. (245)

India for the Indians is represented by an open-air market where, among the profusion of gorgeously colored objects, we also see a bold-looking bazaar woman. She signals the bewilderment caused to the Anglo-Indian imagination when a woman cannot be placed or understood in terms of the domestic sphere. It is from contact with the bazaar and the bazaar women that Englishmen and English values have to be protected. But even here, the liveliness, color, and smells of the bazaar are portrayed lovingly by Croker. As we see later, the bazaar odors come to define a non-English space in the novel—a smell that is revolting, but also a curious lure to the Anglo-Indian imagination. It is a smell that marks a culture, a way of living and being completely closed off from the British inhabitants of Wellunga. The public letter-writer is also a peculiar institution of the Indian bazaar, his presence a reminder of the unequal distribution of literacy in the culture. In Kipling's *Kim*, the letter-writer is an important instrument of communication for Kim's wild plans and schemes. Even his tools signal the difference between the two cultures. When Geoffrey shows Fred Tallboys the old letter from his uncle, Fred recognizes at once the "bazaar paper and bazaar ink" (23) which leads him to conclude that the elder Captain Mallendar had surely "gone native."

It is in this context that the golden-haired Tara is presented as distinctly different from the rest of the General's family in terms that invoke the Victorian hierarchy of racial and cultural types:

> She carried her slight figure with grace, her small stag-like head was set on a long neck, her little proud face was illuminated by a pair of dark granite-gray eyes; she has beautiful taper hands—whilst those of Jessie looked as if her fingers had been cut off at the second joint. (215–16)

Tara's siblings worship her and are placed in a distinctly subordinate position to her because she shows her upper-class English pedigree in her looks and manner. Croker dramatizes the threat to English values in an incident in which Tara's life is threatened by a gigantic man-eating horse which charges at her as she rides through the Indian bazaar. The dangerous Kathiawari horse suddenly decides to attack Tara's horse:

In a second, the Kathiawari was chasing him open-mouthed, and Tara, frantically lashing her Arab, turned to fly; but Rustum was tired, the pursuer fresh, and full of pride and gram. Screaming, and open-mouthed, he drove his prey right to the brink of a deep nullah. Here he intended to overtake and destroy him—for the Kathiawari came of old native stock, who were bred and trained to kill, in the hideous horse-fights so popular with the Rajahs of a bygone time. (253)

This horse evokes the danger and fear associated with the India that lies outside British rule. In a sheer act of perversity, the horse has been "trained to kill" and belongs to a primitive, "bygone" time before the civilizing influence of British rule. Yet Tara represents not middle-class English culture, but in fact, nobility. Her upper-class origins place her above the romantic plot as she signifies British values that are to be honored and protected by the Englishmen who come to India. So Mallendar steps in to save Tara from the Kathiawari horse, injuring himself in the process and earning the status of a hero in the British community.

Before turning to the final episode, I would like to trace the development of the idea of an Englishman "going native" in Croker's fiction through a study of one of her earlier novels, *The Company's Servant* (1908), which gives us another version of the spatial mapping of English and 'other' values. The figure of the degenerate Englishman appears here in the person of Gojar, whose life demonstrates the negative seductions of India. Croker's ambivalence towards the concept of 'going native' is expressed in a range of attitudes from vague uneasiness to a more precise description that is a satiric counterpoint to the pristine confines of Anglo-India. She inherits a Conradian plot of the slow degeneration of the Englishman in the face of the overwhelming influence of the climate, moral atmosphere, and values of the colonies. *Heart of Darkness* is the best-known exemplar of this plot. In her Indian romances, Croker develops this into a more precise description of the consequences of "going native," investing it with gothic horror but not mystic or spiritual degradation, and adding to it either a playful or a sober picture of interracial domesticity. While in the canonical Victorian novel, we never see the culmination of an interracial love plot, Croker imagines the mundane consequences of just such a possibility.

Gojar appears in *The Company's Servant* in Indian garb and takes on an Indian name. He lives with an Indian woman and is addicted to marijuana. Narrating to Vernon, the English hero of the novel, his memories of travels in India while "drifting . . . like a derelict for twenty long years," he describes "not merely its cities, tombs, temples, that the globe-trotter flashes through, nor the trim military cantonments and hill-stations—[but] I know India under the skin—I have learnt the patience, the repose, the stubborn intractability of the East" (163). Gojar goes into gruesome detail as he describes the sacrifice of buffaloes at a festival, which he observed while he was disguised as a native. He then invokes a familiar Victorian image of horrific heathen practices, in this instance of human sacrifice:

> I myself, have seen the dead body of handsome youth, who had been sacrificed to Kali: bled at the wrists and ankles, and disembowelled after the fashion of the ancient augurs; but such a case as that is extremely rare. After human beings, horses were offered, then cattle, as in the Old Testamant, and sheep and goats. Now in most instances the sacrifices have dwindled to a fowl, sweetmeats, and flowers; yet at times of great scarcity, or impending famine, the ancient methods are resumed. (164)

Gojar taps one of the most persistent myths about Eastern religions as a way to mark the extent of his departure from a British norm. The idea of human sacrifice, second only to cannibalism as a cultural myth, establishes the anthropological conception of India most favored by the Anglo-Indians. Gojar's claim that he has encountered, explored, and finally known the unfamiliar marks him as an outcast from his original social group. Croker uses the language of physiognomical transformation, if not the vocabulary of moral shock to convey the consequences of such forbidden knowledge. The transformations wrought by an Indian experience mark the body of the Englishman as surely as they change his character. In a dramatic encounter early in the novel, Vernon saves Gojar from drowning, discovering in the process that Gojar, who appears in every way to be a native, is, in fact, an Englishman. When Vernon visits Gojar's house, he is unable to distinguish Gojar's features from that of a native Indian in the dim light of a lantern: "The thin, finely-cut nose, the haughty piercing eyes, the long, thick beard, surely were those of a Mahomedan from the far North? All classes and races of people drifted up and down, and in and out of a great junction like Tani-Kul." Until Gojar reveals his true identity, Vernon believes he is an Indian. In keeping with its assumptions about the relation between character and land, the novel perpetuates the notion that a certain "native" existence produces its effects on the physiognomy of the Englishman. As Gojar narrates his story, he was once "an officer and a gentleman" (161), but became eventually "the spectacle which people hint at, or discuss with bated breath: an English gentleman who has lost caste, creed, place and name, who has been swept into the Bazaars—and gone under" (171). Gojar looks old and gaunt and is chronically addicted to marijuana when Vernon discovers him.

As a mockingly inverse portrait of an English marriage, Gojar describes his life with Rajee. This Indian woman who keeps house for him is, like him, a social pariah: "Rajee or Mary Ann . . . a withered old hag, half Christian, half heathen" (161). As Gojar gleefully reveals to Vernon, Rajee "has been to London and loves beer; she even drops her h's and we speak the language when we are alone" (161). In marked contrast to Anglo-India, this unconventional domestic arrangement is formed by two people who have crossed cultural, racial, and class boundaries: Gojar passes for a native, while Rajee can pretend to be English working class. Gojar's Indian experiences suggest that the knowledge he gained through contact with sage and charlatan alike took its toll on his restraint and infected him with an addiction to marijuana and a preference for life in the Indian bazaar. Gojar refers to himself as a Satanic figure endowed with forbidden knowledge and lost to the civilized world forever. Croker never makes it clear why Gojar, a brilliant graduate of a British academy, comes to be in this dissipated state, but the reader is given to understand that he was lured by a realm of experience strictly prohibited for the Englishman. However, in the relish with which he presents himself and narrates his experiences we can see Croker advancing to an idea of the pleasures of "going native."

In Old Madras from the very outset invokes the fear that the story of the missing Captain Mallendar must have something to do with a liaison with an Indian woman. When he hears that Mallendar intends to go in search of his uncle, Mr Fleming rattles off a list of possible reasons for his disappearance. These encapsulate the lure of the East as present to the English imagination:

> Oriental life has an irresistible fascination for some natures; the glamour, the relief from convention, and the tyranny of the starched collar, the lure of attractive and voluptuous women, idleness, ease, luxury, drugs! I could tell you of an officer who went crazy about a beautiful Kashmeri, and actually abandoned his regiment and his nationality, in order to live as a native! Twice, his friends came from England to fetch him home, and each time he escaped—even at the eleventh hour in Bombay plunged into the bazaar, hid his identity, and was lost, in every sense! (12)

Croker yokes "luxury" to the lure of Indian women in a way analogous to an addiction to drugs and a forgetfulness of nation and duty. These images of degeneracy associated with a life outside Anglo-Indian society are repeated in a similar sequence in all of Croker's Indian novels. As I discussed earlier, in the Victorian perception, the bazaar is an open promiscuous place that allows the free mingling of races and classes, quite unlike the order, hierarchy, and discipline of an English home. The Indian woman who lures the Englishman away from duty is also associated with the bazaar. As it happens, Captain Mallendar does fall prey to the seductions of India, but in a fairer guise than the bazaar would allow: he falls in love with an Indian princess. However, this transgression does not go unpunished. The fearful maiming that lies at the heart of the novel forms part of a cautionary tale about the perils of departing from English values enshrined in English domesticity.

The Indian woman seems even more central in the domestic life of Captain Mallendar, the missing uncle of Geoffrey Mallendar, than in all the other episodes of the romance. The startling core of the story of Mallendar's uncle captures both Croker's ambivalence towards India and the subversive possibilities of her fiction. Mallendar finds his uncle, disguised as an Indian prince, living with his Indian wife, Alida. Unlike the other Indian women in the story, Alida is not a bazaar woman but a Coorgi princess named 'Puvaka,' who is renamed Alida after she marries Captain Mallendar. She is sixteen when the Captain meets and falls in love with her and finding that his feelings are returned, decides to elope with her to escape the wrath of her family. But Alida's family hear of the plan; ambush the couple; and cut off Captain Mallendar's nose, ears, eyelids, and upper lip. Alida saves his life and nurses him back to health, becoming "his good angel, a miracle of patience and forbearance" (303). Since then, the older Mallendar has been living a life in obscurity completely away from the hub of Anglo-India.

At the climax of the novel, when, at his request, Mallendar's uncle finally unmasks himself before him, we witness the horrible price of interracial love:

> What he beheld was a grey old man, wearing a black skull cap; his withered cheeks were deeply sunken, his scanty beard was white, and oh, the awful noseless face, the bare grinning teeth, the lidless eye-balls,—expressing mute agonised interrogation, and years of hopeless anguish. (305)

As punishment for his breach of social taboos, Captain Mallendar is condemned to hide from society. But he has a comfortable life which is a syncretic combination of British and Indian cultures. The young Mallendar notes that his house is "saturated with novel and aromatic odours" (298). The dark and dimly lit interior of the house has no furniture other than "shadowy divans along the wall, a few rugs on the floor" (298). Captain Mallendar has learned to speak Tamil and Canarese fluently. His English education accounts for his taste in books, choice of food, and his interest in riding, but as he explains to his nephew, he smokes the huka, maintains a royal estate, and has his luxuries "shooting, horses, motors, yes! rupees are a wonderful balm" (304). This version of the romance does not look back to England for its satisfactory conclusion even though for the young Mallendar the price of abandoning England and duty seems almost too great. He thinks of his uncle's fate in all its loss and deprivation, "a young man of his own age, and profession, full of life, energy and expectation, suddenly shut out from his kindred, friends, and nation" (313).

At the heart of the novel lies the body of the mutilated or maimed Englishman, reminiscent of other such figures in English fiction who suffer for their sin of interracial love—Rochester in Charlotte Brontë's *Jane Eyre* and Kurtz of the 'unspeakable' crimes in *Heart of Darkness*, frail and reduced to a voice by the time the narrator finds him. While the former finds redemption through the kind offices of an Englishwoman, the latter is condemned to lose himself in the depths of the Congo. In both cases, the formal closure of the novel is achieved by the elimination of the racial other, Bertha Mason in one case and the gorgeous African woman in the other. *Jane Eyre* affirms the romance plot of a happy 'English' marriage lived out in isolation from English society. The conclusion of Conrad's *Heart of Darkness* is clearly more ambivalent, but with the lie to the Intended, Marlow pays ritual obeisance to the idea of the noble colonizer who remains 'uncorrupted' by his connection to a racial other. Although the racial and cultural other is eliminated, both protagonists have to suffer the tragic consequences of their interracial transgression. Kurtz never returns to Europe, and Rochester and Jane are isolated from English society in Ferndean. Captain Mallender, on the other hand, lives in the same neighborhood as Geoffrey's better-placed cousin Fred, attends Geoffrey's wedding disguised as a native prince, and from the confines of his princely home commands economic and social power.

Croker's fiction depends heavily on similar formal closures: one of the inescapable features of popular romances that is inextricably tied to reader satisfaction. The penniless Mallendar inherits his family estate, marries the pretty, economical, and good-hearted Barbie Miller, and receives many expensive gifts. As Mrs. Nancy Brander says at the very end, "behold, now, he returns leaving crowds of Indian friends . . . and carries away with him a sword, a horse, a fortune, and a bride!" (326). The romance thus wends its way not only back to Anglo-India, but to England. It offers its readers the thrill of vicariously experiencing transgression, yet returning to the safe haven of the familiar. Yet I want to argue that in its attempt to represent the unspeakable, despite its final gesture of repudiation, the romance is more subversive than the canonical English novel. At a very basic level, the romance allows the representation of the native woman within the domestic space, in quotidian relationships, not madly raging in an attic or reduced to an inarticulate image of the African continent. Further, as an examination of the concluding chapters of the novel will show, Croker does not present a neat rejection of India and natives and a fading out of the exotic locale, to be replaced by domestic harmony in England. When Mallendar takes leave of Alida, he is moved by her parting comments: "We heard of you up in Coorg, my country, and in beautiful Mysore. I am your Aunt Alida" (310). Mallendar is confronted with having to acknowledge his kinship with an Indian woman, and Croker describes his pausing to consider this fact, and finally, accepting it: "Mallendar bowed his assent, then as he looked into her face, stirred by an inexplicable impulse, he stooped, and lifted her hand to his lips. Why not? She was his uncle's wife, and she held herself like royalty" (310). This is a critical moment in the romance, when despite the blatant class ideology, Mallendar gives a name to his relationship with this Indian woman who has been the cause of his uncle's disappearance from Anglo-India. Even though the reader is party to Geoffrey's conclusion that despite the sweetness and good humor of Alida, the world of Anglo-India was not well worth losing for a grand passion, and his consequent emotional recoil from his uncle's fate, Croker avoids giving us a pat rejection of India. Alida gets the final words at the parting between her and Mallendar, which establish a kinship between her, the elder Mallendar, and Geoffrey. Looking at his care-worn face and shabby clothes at the end of his adventures, she compassionately comments, "You have had a hard time, but if one leaves the beaten road—one has to pay" (311). In different degrees, they have all left the beaten road, thus establishing kinship with each other.

At Mallendar's wedding to Barbie Miller, the vitriolic Mrs. Fiske notices his 'strange acquaintances' which included "two youths who were almost black" and two other "natives," "a black-bearded man, wearing spectacles, and an immense turban, and a lady who was closely veiled" (324). Though clearly marginalized and shunned by the racist gathering, these guests nevertheless mark the bonds that Mallendar has formed with Major Rochfort's part-Indian family and with his uncle and aunt. The Anglo-Indian romance thus acknowledges the inescapable hybridity of Anglo-Indian life.

III. Readerly Pleasure and the Romance

Most recent studies of Victorian popular fiction emphasize the sheer numbers of novels which are unfamiliar to readers today and which have been neglected by scholarly studies. More importantly, they show the critical consequences of this neglect in our ignorance of the variety of audience response, characters, and themes with which these lesser known authors experimented. There is near unanimity among these scholars that though Victorian popular writers often seem to conform to Victorian narrative conventions, their subversive manipulations or modifications of these norms are equally, if not more significant. Feminist readings of popular fiction point out, for instance, that such fiction could "both endorse and subvert ideological norms in the representation of femininity" (Liggins and Duffy xvii).[15] In the same way, Anglo-Indian fiction both follows and subverts Victorian conventions of representing domesticity. On the one hand it portrays interracial romance as a Gothic aberration and an instance of the perils of stepping out of the boundaries of the British and the familiar; on the other, it dwells in fascination on mixed households and mixed progeny.

We can gather from our reconstruction of the implied readership of the Anglo-Indian romances that like other domestic fiction, these must also have been a powerful method of socialization. As Nancy Armstrong has argued, one of the frames of reference for the domestic novel was conduct books for women, which meant that the novel both produced and represented domestic ideologies (Armstrong 63). Alison Sainsbury describes the novels as seeking to "enfranchise middle-class English women, making them partners—even central agents—in the enterprise of empire" thereby connecting rather than separating public and private spheres (Sainsbury 181). In Croker's *In Old Madras*, however, the perfunctory nature of the conclusion of the marriage and domestic plot complicates the linear progression of desire and readerly pleasure. It coexists in an uneasy relation to the thrill of vicariously going beyond the racial, geographical boundaries of Anglo-India, even if such an experience is only allowed to the Englishman. In this way, Croker's

In Old Madras works both as domestic fiction that participates in the socialization of its readers *and* a fantasy that explores the forbidden realm of interracial love. The Englishman who goes native is punished severely for his transgression, thereby ensuring that the romance has a 'conventional' ending in rejecting miscegenation. However, Croker's readers are placed in the unusual position of condoling yet condoning the grisly punishment of the racially transgressive Englishman. They are also forced to acknowledge that the homely and domestic atmosphere of the other mixed homes outside the social boundaries of Anglo-India are nevertheless intimately connected to it. In its inclusion of Anglo-Indian life, its critique of upper-class British life associated with England and its praise of homeliness even in a mixed home, Croker's romance breaches the boundaries of the unspeakable and complicates the satisfactions of romance.

Part II

Indirect Rule and the Politics of Romance

Anglo-Indian romances articulate a poetics of indirect rule in which themes of negotiation, conciliation, familial ties, and cultural assimilation dominate. Until 1858 the East India Company held sway in India, even though the British government had steadily curtailed its powers.[1] The Mutiny of 1857 raised many questions about England's role in India, but even though there were many contesting opinions about whether or not England should hold on to its colonies, most politicians and statesmen in Victorian England recognized their economic importance.[2] And, as the English laid the groundwork of their economic empire, the belief in colonialism as a "benevolent" force persisted throughout the Victorian period, even among those dissenting voices that considered Britain's expansionist ambitions a drain on national resources. In the case of India, this benevolence ostensibly prompted social reform, directed the annexation of territory, and led to the mid-century introduction of technology in the form of railways and telegraph lines. However, as recent cultural histories of empire have pointed out, only those policies conducive to the protection of British mercantile interests were followed for the social and political amelioration of Indians.³ Sudipta Sen has argued that it was in the process of securing the avenues of commerce and the right to collect revenue that the East India Company became more than a trading company—in effect, trade laid the foundation of a political and economic empire. The liberal aspirations of the Company, therefore, far from being an odd contradiction with its self-interested profit motives, were merely an extension of them.⁴

'Liberal' or benevolent colonial ideas appear as an elaborate and relativist courtesy in the writings of Edmund Burke, but are mainly derived from nineteenth-century political theorists and thinkers such as John Stuart Mill and Jeremy Bentham, who believed in principles of justice and democracy *and* the necessity of imperial control over the colonies. The process of 'reform' and the creation of ideal though not equal citizens of a commonwealth preoccupied colonial administrators such as Lord Dalhousie and Philip Meadows Taylor. It became, in fact, a powerful, seductive fantasy shared by many British colonials of this period. The process of educating Indian subjects is virtually inseparable from British fantasies of creating willing subjects who would desire the rule of a just and democratic nation such as England. This liberal and reformist ideal can be read as a romance narrative in which the success of colonial rule is represented in the figure of the newly educated native who, having recognized its justice, willingly colludes with the British.

The liberal agenda of educating natives was based on a conception of the colonized as children. Rather than see those they ruled as incomprehensibly different, the liberals imagined a kinship with them. The family romance neatly describes these relationships of "kinship" and "tutelage," part of which was the process of educating Indians, which seems to have preoccupied every major liberal thinker in the nineteenth century. This process of education was not confined to social institutions, however; the concept of liberal government itself was conceived of as a gradual process of education. John Stuart Mill, for instance, espoused a utopian ideal of the educative power of government and hence the possibility of overcoming a nation's inherent barbarity. This belief arose from his vision of the progress of civilization and of a world of nations equal in civilization. For him, it was both inevitable and highly desirable that the less civilized country give itself up gladly to its more civilized conqueror, "rather than to sulk on his own rocks, the half-savage relic of past times, revolving in his own little mental orbit, without participation or interest in the general movement of the world" (Mill 363). Mill clearly viewed such a conquest as a triumph of the cosmopolitan expansion of the world, a refusal to participate in which was an act of petulant isolationism.

The contradictions that confronted liberal thinkers and colonial rulers in India were inherent in liberalism itself. Uday Mehta points out that it is not a mere accident that liberals were so centrally involved in questions of colonial governance; rather, their interest in colonialism was a logical derivation from liberal ideas. His analysis of liberal political ideology is especially pertinent to an understanding of family romance and also explains its peculiar form in British India. The family is a particularly apposite concept for framing a study of liberalism because "as something starkly hierarchical and governed by a paterfamilias whose authority is not quite political but who has the power of 'commanding and chastising' his children [it] is that essential penumbra on which the political thought of liberalism relies" (Mehta 33). Liberalism always recognized the stranger as a "familiar, though deformed, double," the "child/deviant, whose difference threatens the legitimacy of the father by placing a limit on the reach of his authority" (Mehta 33). The resolution offered is assimilation into the family which is "adjacent to the political sphere" and where power can be used with fewer constraints (Mehta 33).

The complexity and often contradictory nature of these paternal, "benevolent" imperatives finds one of its clearest expressions in the conditions of indirect rule. While veneration for hereditary aristocracy and its cultural authority made a policy of appeasement the obvious choice for British rulers, the gains to be had from territorial annexation also influenced colonial policy. The Company and its representatives set up a vast disciplinary regime which organized, regulated, and scrutinized both the personal lives of rulers and their public policies. Victorian patriarchy assumed a new form in its supervisory and socializing functions vis-à-vis the native princes. The paternal benevolence that underlay British policy is clearly expressed in declarations of political intent by administrators in both the early and later part of the century. The influential 'foursome of Scots'—Thomas Munro (Governor of Madras 1820–26), John Malcolm (Governor of Bombay 1827–30), Montstuart Elphinstone (Governor of Bombay 1819–27), and Charles Metcalfe (Resident at Hyderabad 1820–25)—were the chief proponents of indirect rule in India (Zastoupil 59). Malcolm, describing the ideal interaction with the Mahratta prince of Guicowar, writes: "We may give advice when required. We may express regret when we conceive he errs, and be forward to testify our delight when his measures merit approbation; but nothing short of danger to the public peace should lead to any other interference" (Malcolm 14). This careful edifice of shared authority was necessary to keep up appearances and to find allies through whom indirect rule could be maintained. Malcolm's principles for dealing with the prince of Guicowar sound like paternal injunctions to socialize a son. The idea of benevolent colonialism made such a paternal relation likely, but it was manifested materially in the concrete divisions of economic and social responsibilities between the British government and the native elite such as supervision of the education of royal heirs, protecting the women, approving household expenditure, and providing pensions for the dependents of royal families.

The paternal relationship between British colonials and Indian rulers also meant that the latter were often feminized and infantilized. Many of the native princes were considered unfit for 'good rule' because they lacked Victorian 'masculine' virtues thought essential for a good ruler. The Indian domestic sphere, usually conflated with the harem, was seen as the source of an emasculating influence that prevented the native princes from the "manly" discharge of public duties. This sense of the enervating influence of the private life of the kings seems a clear departure from the Victorian notion of separate spheres in which the protected space of the home has an ennobling influence on the man who functions in the public realm. "Oriental" domesticity, by contrast, has only a negative influence on the public domain of politics. In the case of women rulers, indirect rule led to political conflict which often took the form of domestic drama. This was not merely a figure of speech but also a social-political arrangement by which British Residents often supervised domestic arrangements for the widows of kings who had died without heirs. In chapters 3 and 4, I explore how this colonial relationship is complicated by the fact that Indian women were both rulers and subjects of the East India Company.

Indirect rule came about as a peculiar form of government in colonial India because from the very beginning the Company Directors and the British government were in favor of restraint when it came to political expansion in India. Even as late as Governor-General Wellesley's tenure (1798–1805), not all British policy makers agreed with his aggressive annexations and Wellesley was recalled to England (Fisher, "Politics" 18). From the Company's point of view, the annexations became inevitable once its mercantile interests got inextricably involved with the revenue and administrative functions of already existing governments. British policy evolved from a principle of noninterference in the affairs of native states (which directed only reluctant takeover of territory) to a partial or complete control of administrative and revenue functions. Hence, the annexation of princely states during Lord Dalhousie's tenure as Governor-General did not so much mark a shift in British policy on the question of territorial acquisition as give it a decisive shape. In the years after Dalhousie's assumption of office in 1847, Sambalpur, Satara, Jhansi, Nagpur, The Punjab, and Oudh were annexed, giving the British a real stake in setting up large and efficient bureaucracies. Earlier Governor-Generals like Wellesely and the Marquess of Hastings had realized that British commercial interests could only be secured by ensuring political stability in the states adjoining British territories. By bringing many of the large states under British rule, Dalhousie's policies laid the ground for the establishment of British administration, public works, and large bureaucracies in different parts of India.

The annexation of the native states was accomplished under the quasi-legal rubric of 'Paramountcy,' a unique configuration of political relationships peculiar to the British empire in India.[5] The term was used to designate a political relationship between the colonizing power and the princely states which secured for the colonizing power the military, police, and revenue functions of government, and which steadily eroded the power of the princely states, transforming them from independent or semi-independent to dependent, subordinate or feudatory states.[6] It is clear that there was no uniform relation with the princely states to begin with because any such relation had to take a large number of variable factors into account. These included the strategic importance of a state to the British, its level of hostility or friendship, its perceived wealth, and its administrative infrastructure.

Since the British perception of itself as following the rule of law rather than the despotic principles of native princes was so important to its self-definition, the administrators wanted to give Paramountcy the form of a legitimate system of law that could be quoted as precedent. As Ian Copland explains, 'rule of law' was "a commitment to principle and precedent, to administration by regulation rather than whim or expediency" (Copland 212). But given the disparity between the different states, this was precisely what they could not do. Each state had to be dealt with on its own terms and with special reference to the history of its relations with the Company. By the late nineteenth century, it was quite clear to British officials that *realpolitik* and political expediency governed their relations with the native states. Even though officials with political experience such as William Lee-Warner and Charles Tupper, and a legal theorist such as John Westlake, wrote copiously to create the category of 'Indian Political Law,' it was "a strange mixture of contract, usage, interpretation and legislation" (Copland 214).

The Resident or Political Agent was one of the key actors in the process of bringing about gradual administrative control of the colonies. The appointment of the first Resident in 1764 marked the transition for the British from being a commercial force to becoming a political power. After 1858, when the British government took over administration of its Indian colony, the Resident became even more important in the administrative and diplomatic affairs of the states. His administrative and diplomatic powers grew with the development of colonial rule. Initially Indian rulers considered receiving a British Resident at the court an honor and a mark of the Company's favor towards them. They, in turn, sent *wakils* (attorneys) as mediators, facilitators, and informants to the Presidencies. But the complex relationship between the Resident, the ruler, the subjects of the state in question and its past relationship with the Company meant that there was constant maneuvering and jostling for power between the Company and the ruler. In the early to mid-nineteenth century, Indian rulers tried to control and restrict the functions of the Residency. Michael Fisher lists bribing, discrediting, evading, and placating Residents as the strategies most commonly used to contain the power of the Residents. Initially the rulers succeeded in frustrating the plans of the Resident to supervise administration in the state, and a powerful ruler such as Mahadaji Scindia called the shots for a very long time. But as the Company grew in power, the rulers were unable to control the power of the Residents.[7] Emphasizing the importance of the Resident to a new kind of rule, Ian Copland points out that "nothing is more striking in the history of the Indian feudatory policy than the rise to prominence, in the 1870's, of the men on the spot. Accelerated promotion in the decades after the Mutiny, a tightening up of recruitment following the establishment of the Staff Corps in 1861, and the injection of new blood in the form of competition civilians . . . made a vast difference to the *esprit de corps* of the Political Service." (Copland 130).

The two chapters in this section deal directly with indirect rule and hence narratives involving political struggle between British Residents and Indian rulers. In chapter 3, the Ranis of annexed states play disaffected daughters of the Company and point out that it has betrayed its obligation to protect and rescue them. In this case, the trope of rescue is used by these women to remind the Company that it is not acting as the liberal power it purports to be. At the same time, the Ranis are engaged in a political struggle with the Company and disputes about control of territory and property and the succession and education of male children dominate these quasi-familial exchanges. The language of familial civility plays out a family romance even as it is subverted in the rebellion of good daughters against the paternal wishes of the British Resident.

In chapter 4, I argue that romance writer and colonial official Philip Meadows Taylor struggles to make the recalcitrant Rani of Berar compliant to British authority, a process he recounts with brutal frankness in his letters. The British colonial here is not the benevolent savior of the Indian damsel in distress; in fact, as I show in my reading of Taylor's letters, he mocks the language of chivalry. As the head of a besieged subsidiary state, the Rani of Shorapur initially treats Taylor as head of the household and state. However, these political relations change dramatically when the Rani protests bitterly against the British and questions their benevolence. It is only in his own fictional universe, *Seeta*, which is at the same time a domestic drama, interracial love story, and political allegory, that Taylor can produce an educable and compliant Indian heroine. Taken together, Taylor's memoir, political letters, and fiction show that while the historical Rani of Shorapur was an unruly recalcitrant political opponent, in his ideal imagined universe, the Indian woman was pliant and domestic.

CHAPTER THREE

Family Quarrels
The Royal Widows and the East India Company

British colonial writers often transformed their belief in the educative powers of government into a romance about turning natives into political allies. In this version of the romance, political opponents could be cast in familial roles, particularly when they were women and subject to colonial and native patriarchy. When these women remained recalcitrant, however, the romance reached a crisis and transformed them into immoral or corrupt opponents and the paternal figure of the Resident into a cruel oppressor. A perfect example of this type of narrative was the case of the widowed queens or Ranis of native Indian states whose territory lapsed to the British government between 1848 and 1856. The annexation of the central Indian state of Jhansi aroused popular interest in England when the heroic Rani Lakshmibai of Jhansi rode into battle against British forces during the Mutiny of 1857. The Ranis of three other states—Nagpur, Satara, and Sambalpur—less known and less celebrated, were similarly placed vis-à-vis the East India Company. Initially figureheads and regents for their adopted heirs, these Ranis refused to be educated into obedient subjects. Instead, they launched a series of protests against the decisions of the East India Company regarding their estates, pensions, household expenses, and their customary right to adopt a son and heir. Departing from the usual focus on the silently victimized Indian widow, this episode in nineteenth-century history shows the upper-class widow as a politically militant figure, in the midst of domestic chaos, and embroiled in a conflict about property.

After the annexations of their states, these widows became dependents of the Company which became responsible for the disposal of their property, allocation of their pensions, and regulation of their daily expenditure. Even though the British Resident was a potentially hostile figure, he personally supervised arrangements for the queens, maintained cordial relations with the ruling family, and often lived on the same estate. The negotiations between the widowed queens and the Resident thus became inevitably familial. He did his best to turn them into good daughters and loyal subjects in a family romance even as they defied the roles imposed on them. It is indicative of the convolutions of this family romance that even though the conflict over property and power had all the features of a marital dispute, the Ranis played on the popular designation of the Company as a father figure and described themselves as its daughters. Even their protests against the decisions of the Company are couched in the language of familial betrayal. For instance, when the Ranis of Nagpur complained to the Commissioner of Nagpur about the conduct of a British official who interfered with the organization of the women's quarters, they said, "we are your daughters, and you are our father . . . we have no protector but you" (qtd. in Rahim 260). The Resident, however, assumed those responsibilities of the absent husband or Raja such as organizing the household and monitoring expenses. It is thus an incestuous economy in which good daughters could also occupy the place of obedient wives.

The language of civility, the invocation of familial relations, the address to the Company as protector are all conventions of the exchange between the Ranis and the Company that are quite consistently followed in the correspondence between the two. Yet the elaborate convention that, on the one hand, keeps in place the paternal structures of authority becomes, on the other, the vehicle for articulating the failure of paternal authority to guarantee the happiness of the good daughters and wives. As Michael Fisher has pointed out in the case of the remarkable Begum Samru, who became a powerful landowner and power-broker under Company rule, she "used kinship terms for her relationships with British officials," though this was not reciprocal because in a 'rational-bureaucratic' system, the Company wanted to avoid reference to personal ties in public matters ("Becoming" 107). As I show in the final section of this chapter, the hero of the Mutiny, the Rani of Jhansi, maintains the language of familial civility in her pleas to the Company that her adopted son be recognized as the new ruler. In that sense, the romance of good subject/paternal ruler is played by both sides. However, the subsequent actions of the Rani show decisively that there is a counternarrative that was equally visibly played out and that exposed the romance of indirect rule. In folklore and Hindi literature, the Rani became a symbol not of compliance, but its opposite: she was seen as a hero of the first war of independence against British rule.

Historical accounts of the annexations represent these women as victims of the self-interested policies of the Company and the uncompromising stance of Governor-General Dalhousie. Colonial accounts, on the other hand, represent the Ranis as obstructors of the true cause of justice who had to be summarily pensioned off, or else as disobedient daughters who were misled by bad advisors to make unjust demands in defiance of the paternal designs of the Company. Historians of the period have not sufficiently highlighted the implications of the Company's frequent use of "doctrine of lapse," a policy that denied to rulers the right both to inherit and administer their estates and to adopt heirs, specifically in the case of women rulers. These policies of annexation were critically assessed in light of the fact that the Revolt of 1857 was popularly understood as having been caused by Dalhousie's ruthless annexation of Indian states during his tenure from 1848 to 1856.[1]

It is strange that these women should stay marginal to this history given that they brought to a crisis questions about takeover of territory, the definition of public and private property, the ideology of separate spheres, and class-based notions of gender and public power. Given their marginality, it is easy to forget that they were actors in a crucial episode in the establishment of British rule in India—the transition from indirect rule through Residents to direct annexation of territory by the East India Company. Administrative documents that record the suppression of women regents, or potential heads of state, can be read for the contradictions that they expose in the idea of benevolent rule. The rhetoric of social reform, bringing modernity to pre-industrial India, and the provision of a more humane and hence more civilized dispensation to the Indian woman were an essential part of the fantasy of good rule. The constant reminders that the British were snatching away the rights of the widows of princely states sat uncomfortably against this rhetoric. It worked against the notion that they were saviors of the Indian woman, a fiction that was central to their sense of themselves as benevolent rulers engaged in a civilizing mission. In reading the Ranis as potentially subversive, I am not suggesting that they presented self-conscious critiques of patriarchy or imperialism. It is important to note, however, that their resistance to the quiet life of obscurity that was being forced on them projected them from a life of seclusion into a more militant public and political role.

The self-justification of the Company is a key to understanding the rhetorical and ideological battles between the Ranis and the Company. By the early nineteenth century British colonialism distinguished itself from other forms of conquest and from "Oriental Despotism" by its concern with rule of law and with due process. In British self-perception, one of the markers of their enlightened rule was their intercession on behalf of the widow, and the banning of Sati and other "barbaric" practices in British ruled states. This belief became so well established that it persisted into the late colonial period. Indeed, in 1894, William Lee-Warner, Political Secretary in the Bombay Residency, described "Native administrations" as conducted "in a different spirit from our own" and characterized by the fact that "infanticide, suttee, and the burning of witches continued to be practiced and honoured just over an imaginary border, long after their suppression within the territories governed by British law" (*Protected Princes* 19). Company officials were especially concerned that native rulers and their subjects, and the British Parliament and people perceive their negotiations with the queens as part of a larger "civilizing mission" undertaken with the consent of the governed.

The Gender of Good Rule

East India Company policies in eighteenth-century India were centered largely on deliberations about the ownership of land, the question being whether it rested with the Mughal emperor or with the landowner. It was believed that imperial authority was limited to rent, not ownership of property. Warren Hastings, Philip Francis (Supreme Councillor in Bengal 1774–80), and finally Cornwallis (Governor-General of India, 1786–93) are only the best known in a long line of policy makers who dueled with custom and usage and the authority of written texts among Muslims and Hindus to finally establish the primacy of English law in the matter of legislating land revenues and ownership of landed property. In a recent study of colonial ideology, Robert Travers argues for a more nuanced perception of the deliberate process by which the British under Warren Hastings, and before, negotiated between Mughal law, custom, local usage, their own sense of 'ancient constitutionalism,' and their brand of Whiggish ideas. This process of engagement with Indian aristocracy and traditional scholars like maulvis and pundits on the question of land rights was a distinctive feature of indirect rule in India. For my purposes, the most striking aspect of these negotiations, which undoubtedly created great confusion and consternation, is that it was often women landowners whose rights were infringed by Company legislation. Thus it is they who publicly challenged the Company's ideas about laws of inheritance, the place of women in segregated societies, and the ability of women to negotiate their claims to property.[2]

Until very recently, this fact received scant attention in histories of the period even though the colonial record is full of pleas, protests, and petitions from women rulers of small states and women landowners. In demonstrating the kinds of judgments the Company courts were compelled to give for land disputes, the confrontation with women landholders reveals the elaborate rhetorical moves and fictions the Company was compelled to invent about protecting secluded women. An example of the nature of this clash over property between widows and the Company can be seen as early as 1776 in the case of Nauderah Begum, whose claim to her deceased husband's property was disputed by his nephew, Bahadur Beg, even though she claimed full inheritance on the basis of a deed of gift and a record of the actual transfer of property. Bahadur Beg took his claim to the Company's provincial council in the town of Patna where traditional Muslim legal scholars like the qazis and Muftis were asked to express their opinions, which they offered, arguing that only one-fourth of the property could be given to the Begum for her maintenance. The Begum refused to submit to the judgment of the Council and fled to a nearby Islamic religious compound, taking her documents with her. She then appealed to the Supreme Court in Calcutta to intervene.[3] Chief Justice Elijah Impey's subsequent judgment was less a defense of the Begum's right to inherit property than a reprimand to the provincial court for having delegated its authority to Muslim qazis and muftis.[4] Both English and native patriarchy thus tried to disinherit women and undermine their abilities.[5] Evidence from the period indicates that women had been landowners, or had acted as proxies for sons or male heirs. Naudhera Begum's actions suggest that she did have a sense of legal process and legal rights and was capable of functioning in the public sphere. Betty Joseph interprets the disqualification of female landholders from 1776 to 1789 as evidence that the 'secluded woman' of Oriental societies had become "the limit case for English law" since she could not be produced in court or exposed to the public eye (Joseph 144). Yet, as Joseph points out, the Ranis of Rajshahi and of Burdwan, even though they were secluded, had been able to conduct the business of their estates and their correspondence with the Company and the courts through their agents. The Rani of Burdwan possessed enough insight into legal and bureaucratic processes to understand that there was tension between the commercial and legal wings of the colonial state, that is, between the East India Company and the Supreme Court, which she then astutely exploited in her petitions.[6]

In the case of Nauderah Begum, Elijah Impey of the Supreme Court intervened with a decision against the Company courts, invoking the 'hapless widow' in support of his argument. Striking the chivalric note which later became the keynote of Edmund Burke's speeches against Hastings, Impey expressed horror at the oppression of the widow and the mistreatment she had received at the hands of Company officials. Both Impey and the Muslim legal scholars thus thought of Indian women as dependents, unable to act on their own, and hence unfit to inherit property. Criticizing Impey's imposition of English law, George Bogle, the 'Commissioner of Law Suits,' argued in favor of Muslim law as interpreted by the qazis, and ironically, accused the English court of having subjected a 'secluded woman' to the mortification of having to appear in court! For both sides, the rhetoric of 'saving the widow' undergirded the argument for the humanity and superiority of the laws they supported (Travers 198–203). It is precisely this inflammatory rhetoric and these ideological positions focused on the figure of the disinherited widow that came to have such power in political battles for the next half century of colonial rule.

The inheritance of property became an even more contentious issue for widows of kings in the case of native states without male heirs. The ambiguity of the law and the great variety of local practices regarding widow remarriage, especially their right to inherit and retain the property of their deceased husbands, became a controversial issue among British and Indian reformers, culminating in the passing of the Hindu Widows Remarriage Act of 1856. In the Panjab, for instance, customary law allowed the Hindu widow to inherit property in the absence of male lineal descendents, but because she could then alienate her share for economic reasons, alarmed British officials felt it necessary to take action prohibiting the partition of land. British colonials were interested in keeping village communities intact by supporting traditional landowners, which often meant restricting the widow's right to inherit or dispose of land.[7] British jurists invoked custom, usage, scripture, and Victorian patriarchy in arbitrary ways to codify and make uniform a diverse body of personal and property law and this argument between pre-colonial practices and Victorian legislation came to a head in the case of the royal widows. Even though these were royal widows rather than impecunious women fighting for their property, they managed to make the Company look like a persecutor rather than protector of the widows. The precedent of other annexations, especially Oudh, and disputes about inheriting estates that appear over and over again in the colonial record had made the protection of the widow a sentimental issue. The Ranis could and did play on this fact. The conflict over property also has to be situated in the context of British perception of the Ranis which was directed by Victorian ideologies of gender and their relation to private and public space. The annexations also brought to the fore the clash between these ideologies and the Ranis' understanding of their rights and entitlements.

I present four case studies here, which are arranged so as to make clear the structural similarities between all four instances of the drama of annexation in the states of Satara, Nagpur, Sambalpur, and Jhansi. The Ranis in each of these states use similar strategies of resistance, play up their maternal or familial roles, and remind the British of their historical status as their loyal subjects. The polygamous Rajas of Nagpur and Sambalpur left four wives each, but the protests against the provisions made for them were usually led by the eldest and chief Rani. Inevitably, the British representatives suspected the Ranis of being disloyal, questioned their right to property, and commented on their immorality. As British colonial writings make clear, the Ranis were called upon to become regents or chose to become rulers, often against the political designs of the Company. Although each of these states had different historical and political circumstances, and the British no uniform relationship with them, their treatment of the Ranis was without exception the same: they were reduced to figureheads or considered incapable of ruling the state, pensioned off, and forced into retirement.

SATARA

The annexation of Satara in Western India became so controversial that it was discussed in British Parliament. The past political loyalty of Raja Pratap Singh had given the Company no reasonable excuse to take over the state. The eldest Rani Rajas Bai's ability to rule was discussed both by the Raja and the Company. Rajas Bai entered the political stage when the male line of the royal family died without leaving behind a natural heir in 1847, though he had adopted a son before he died. The fortunes of Satara had been uncertain for many decades before Pratap Singh was brought out of captivity and placed on the throne in 1819. The Raja and the Company signed a treaty of perpetual friendship and alliance, which promised sovereignty to the heirs and successors of the king. However, the Company took charge of military protection of his territory, his political relations, and general supervision of his administration. Pratap Singh retained the support of the Company until he became restless under his dependent status. Once Resident Briggs began to interfere in the administration of the state, relations between the Raja and the Company deteriorated rapidly. The Raja was deposed in 1839 and his younger brother Appa Sahib made king. The Rani's troubled relationship with the Company was simply the aggravation of a long-standing conflict that had begun in the time of Pratap Singh, but again, it assumed its peculiar form only when a woman ruler entered the picture. The Rani was as disempowered by the injunctions of native patriarchy as she was by the British perception of women as unfit rulers. In a letter to his deputy Rungo Bapoojee, her husband, Raja Pratap Singh, writes:

> As long as I am spared, there may be nothing very much to dread; but in the event of my death, my two Ranees will have to be guarded against all machinations, in consequence of their incompetency, as females, to understand affairs of state, and owing to the possibility of their being tampered with and imposed upon. . . . Whatever difficulty may arise with respect to the possibility of the Princesses being unfairly dealt with, you must be prepared, if you are alive, to grapple with and remove. You must be on your guard against any papers or oral communications which may purport to proceed from them, directly at variance with my own interests, or contradictory to their duties to me. You are fully aware that what is pretended to emanate from females or minors, is neither legal nor valid. (qtd. in Basu 295)

In pointing to the deceptions that can be practiced upon the Ranis, the Raja's words emphasize the politically charged rhetoric of the helplessness of women rulers. According to both British and Indian patriarchal conceptions, the Ranis were incapable of holding political power and would not be able to understand affairs of state. Yet the fear that the widows of princely states could hold political power as regents or with the help of advisors convinced the British to neutralize them by giving them pensions and forcing them into a life of retirement away from the political centers of their states.

Between the injunctions of native patriarchy and the assumptions of the colonial state, the Ranis seem to have been passive instruments in the war of succession. However, that is not how they appear in all historical accounts, some of which point out that people were struck by the Queen Mother's confident presence when she rode her horse like a man; talked freely to men who approached her; and looked more in command than her son, the prince (Basu 22). The struggle for political power between Rani Saguna Bai and the Company took the indirect medium of negotiating a personal, religious, and customary right such as the right to adopt a son. But even though custom enjoins the adoption of a son who would succeed to the throne, the Rani actively campaigns from the position of the regent and queen mother. In her petitions to the Government, she pushes for sovereignty on her own behalf as much as for her son. At first, she seems to concede the demands of the British government, but then clings tenaciously to her own demands on the crucial question of adoption. In a letter to Major Stewart, Secretary to the Government of India, she asks for clemency from the British government, given that the reasons "which led . . . to the loss of our country are unknown to us poor women" (qtd. in Basu 289). In such a statement, the Rani uses the rhetorical force of their helpless female status at the same time that she asks for political power. She claims that she knows nothing about matters of state, but is in the peculiar position of being involved in every decision involving the state. In his cover letter, Major Stewart gives his own response to the Rani's petition:

> The above resolution has been the result of much deliberation on the Rani's part, and may be considered entirely her own act and deed. To assure myself that she perfectly understood the contents, the paper was carefully read over and explained to her in my presence, after which she delivered it to me with her own hands, stating that she left the case entirely to the mercy and consideration of the British government. (Basu 290)

But though in this memorandum the Rani withdrew her claim to the throne, she insisted that the adoption of a son was a religious duty which she could not give up. In these negotiations with the Company, the Rani is both a helpless dependent and political antagonist, deprived of the power to make decisions but called upon to take a stand on political issues. The Resident, Major Stewart, is impressed by the Rani's strong resolve: "After considerable discussion on this subject, I left the Rani's presence impressed with her conviction that her objections to disclaim the adoption of the boy are insuperable. She is passionately attached to him and will hear of no compromise by which the fact of adoption is called into question" (qtd. in Basu 290). The Rani uses maternal affection as a fundamental nonnegotiable right even if it goes against the political objectives of the Company. She presents herself to the Resident as a mother claiming her rights rather than as the ruler of a state in conflict with British rule. Both parties are aware, however, that the adoption of a son is a highly political issue.

The long conflict and the tense relations between the Company and the royal family of Satara takes on a new form when the Rani represents the conflict in familial terms, laced with expectation, betrayal, and appeals such as a daughter would make to a father or guardian. The overt paternalism of this relation might seem typical in the context of the protracted negotiations between the Company and the native rulers, but the correspondence between Dalhousie and the Rani enacts once again a family romance created by conditions in which a domestic woman might assume political power. In her letters to the Governor-General and Secretary of State for India, the Rani assumes the position of wronged subject, ill-treated ally, deprived mother, and legal petitioner. In her first letter, which was sent to the Government of Bombay and to Her Majesty's Secretary of State for India, she writes of the betrayal of her confidence by the Company:

> ... and that Company, I was perfectly confident, would honourably render me assistance as an ally in case any wicked power through ill will should be inclined to deprive me of my sovereignty and would protect me like a turtle dove. Instead of this, I say, that Honourable Company was bent upon falling on their own ally and thus gratifying their greed like a cruel tigress that falls upon her own offspring to appease her hunger. (qtd. in Basu 273)

The Rani states the relation of filial dependence in which she stands to the Company and her expectation that they would protect her. At the same time, she also describes herself as a political ally of the Company. Her image of the turtle dove protecting her young frames her relationship with the Company as a question of familial affection rather than state diplomacy. Further, the Company is figured as a maternal and nurturing power that commits the unnatural act of turning on its own young. The Rani's letter plays on the British rhetoric about its status as a protective and dependable sovereign power with obligations of a feudal nature towards its dependants. Her political negotiations with the Company and their betrayal of their obligations to her are thus represented as a failure of personal, familial relations.

The expectations of the Rani of Satara were, not surprisingly, in conflict with what the Company was prepared to allow her when the question of a pension came up. In his minute of 7 August 1850, Dalhousie judged the expectations of the Rani to be too high. He acted on the advice of the Resident who suggested "that a stipend should be granted of Rs 5000 a month, which he considers would be sufficient for the maintenance of the whole family, although it would be far short of the Rani's hopes and wishes" (qtd. in Basu 295). This wrangling over personal expenses and the household establishment has all the features of a family quarrel. However, it was also more than that because it implied control not only over the Rani's household and domestic space, but also over all the marks of her social and political status.

The struggle over appropriate pension for the Rani of Satara thus did not remain a question of household organization, but in fact, took on a political color when it came up for discussion in British Parliament. The Satara controversy caused concern and consternation because the government was anxious that the British not appear as ruthless, despotic rulers. Questions regarding the justice of the annexation, the provisions made for the Ranis, and concern for its influence on the people of India were raised by concerned members of Parliament. Sympathizers of the Company argued that the Rani's complaint about the inadequacy of the provisions made for her was really a front for her grievance regarding the Company's refusal to allow her to adopt a son. While the court considered the provisions made for her liberal, the Rani, "under the influence of her advisors," rejected it as too meager for her needs. In this case, none of the Ranis pursued the matter but accepted "the meagre and poor allowance on the execution of a renunciation of all claims" to the principality of Satara (Rahim 19). The Rani's refusal to accept the offer of a pension was read as strategy, as rebellion, as an act of disloyalty potentially threatening to the British government. When the case of the Raja of Satara came up for discussion in the British Parliament, a member reported that the Rani had refused the stipend and insisted on putting forward her adopted son as the rightful heir of Satara. When another member asked if the money owing to the Rani had been paid to her, he responded that though the money had been repeatedly offered, she had refused to give a receipt for it (Parliamentary Debates 3rd series. 107: 1156).

NAGPUR

In the case of the Central Indian state of Nagpur, Dalhousie's dismissal of the chief queen Banka Bai's claim to the throne restates both Victorian and Hindu orthodoxies about lineage and descent. When the conflict between the Government of India and the Ranis escalated, Dalhousie is reported to have told Banka Bai that "she was not at all the representative of the Bhonsle family by any law, custom, or precedent, European, Maratha or Hindu" (Rahim 249). Of course, this was not an issue when the Company needed her as a quasi-figurehead—then they simply ignored traditional injunctions against a woman assuming political power.

Banka Bai of Nagpur became regent for her son Parsaji after the death of her husband Raghuji II, but was replaced soon after by the son of the king's younger brother, Appa Sahib, who was supported by the Maratha chiefs. Appa Sahib lost favor with the British when he was found intriguing with other small states and kingdoms in the region. He was deposed and another maternal grandson of Raghuji II was adopted by Banka Bai and chosen as heir to the throne. He became Raghuji III, and in 1818, at the age of ten, was placed on the throne of Nagpur. By a treaty of 1826, "his territories were guaranteed to the Raja, his heirs, and his successors" (Rahim 218). Banka Bai was made the head of the regency and given charge of his person, the court, and his household. The British government controlled various departments in his name. A period of efficient administration followed, and the Raja seems to have stayed in the good books of the British for the next seventeen years under the "fatherly care" of Resident Jenkins, who wrote a very favorable report on the state of the kingdom and of the young king (Rahim 218).

In 1850, the then Resident Davidson stated that the Raja had not attended to business for years, had been taking part in irresponsible wars, and had brought the state to a condition of economic bankruptcy. This neglect was perceived in the standard images in which a 'decadent' aristocracy was portrayed in British official records. Making the usual colonial association between tyranny, sensuality, and indolence, Charles Jackson, a contemporary British official, quotes from a report of Resident Mansel from 1853 which states that the Raja of Nagpur was addicted to "the low pleasures of the harem," where he spent his time absorbed in the "paltry conversation and the mean pursuits of the concubines" (qtd. in Jackson 21). He reports further that "a concubine, by name Janee, is spoken of as having led the Rajah into confirmed habits of drinking about eight years since, so that now, when not ill, his drinking exceeds a bottle of brandy a day. Not a few disgraceful scenes have occurred at the palace while the Raja has been overcome with spirits, and generally it may be said that indisposition has thus grown into incapacity to discharge business in the thoughtful and earnest form becoming, for any continuance of time" (qtd. in Jackson 25). Instead of attending to matters of state, the Raja was said to have engaged himself in "the sports of wrestling, kite-flying, and cards, in singing and dancing, and in the intercourse of his dancing-girls" (qtd. in Jackson 25).

In a similar vein, William Lee-Warner, Political Secretary in Bombay in 1894, criticizing Lord Cornwallis's reservations about British expansion in India, reiterates a moral and masculine idea of government upheld by the British and opposed to "despotism":

> In this policy he miscalculated the conditions of Asiatic society, and overlooked the consideration that Empires must rest on moral foundations . . . the development of good and progressive government required the counterpoise of a Church, a nobility, or free institutions, of which, except in the Panjab, hardly any germ existed. If despotism was the only possible form of Native government, it was essential that it should be beneficent; but the immoral influences of the Zenana, and of a Court surrounded by flattery and intrigue, were destructive of a wholesome "tone of empire," and opposed to the idea of any duty or mission. (Lee-Warner, *Protected Princes* 97)

Both Jackson and Lee-Warner articulate a Victorian masculine idea of good government that is disassociated from the women's world of luxury and indolence. But at the same time that the influence of women made a king unfit for martial and administrative duties, it was also a dangerous political influence feared by British administrators. Their suspicion of the zenana arose from the fact that queens and women of the household took active part in nominating a successor to the throne. As Indrani Chatterjee makes clear, matriarchs did have important political functions in the household through adoption and raising of children, and even involvement in political strategy.[8]

The question of Banka Bai's continuing as regent arose when Raghuji III died in 1853, leaving behind four wives but no natural or adopted heir. The British Resident Mansel reported that it had been the Raja's decision to forgo his right to adopt a son, but the chief minister to the king maintained that the Company had not responded to the king's petitions to be allowed to adopt a son. Since successive Residents had differed widely in their opinions about what should be done with the state of Nagpur, Mansel suggested a compromise by which the seventy-five-year-old Banka Bai would rule the country as she was "a superior woman of good feelings and good sense, and possessed high personal character" (Rahim 221). The Resident would not interfere, but would oversee the administration of the state, and the government would reserve the right to cancel the grant in the event of the Bai being too incapacitated to satisfactorily perform her duties. He also recommended the adoption of the grandson of a sister of the Raja, a young boy called Yashwant Rao Ahir Rao, who had received special attention from the late Raja. Banka Bai was to continue as Regent for a few years until he came into his own and was ready to take charge of the state. Mansel believed that such an arrangement "would conciliate the prejudices of the native aristocracy and would satisfy the people" (Rahim 222). Banka Bai, the widow of Raghuji II, was thus placed in the peculiar position of being both ally and antagonist (if she decided to assert her independent claim to the throne), both figurehead and powerful regent.

Dalhousie disagreed with Mansel's recommendations and saw no reason to preserve the Bhonsle line or the state of Nagpur, especially as the strategic benefits to be derived from acquiring Nagpur were considerable. Geographically, it would connect Bombay and Calcutta, providing easier access to two of the major Presidencies. It would be a rich source of revenue and raw cotton that fed the British textile industry in Manchester. But with all his aggressively pragmatic beliefs, Dalhousie tried to conceal the expediency of the annexation by saying that "British rule was a blessing to the agriculturists, bankers, shopkeepers, and lower orders" and "would be preferred by all classes including nobles and even Ranis" (Rahim 225). The officials of the Company desired that popular opinion in India and England continue to perceive the Company as a benevolent ruler, and the best way to achieve this end was by a show of concern for the subject population of Nagpur. In order to take over the state, it was necessary to make the case that Nagpur was badly administered and that Banka Bai was unfit to rule.

When Dalhousie decided to annex Nagpur, he argued that succession was only possible through the male line, and Nagpur had none. Also, Banka Bai's age, which had earlier earned her the respect of the British, now made her incapable of ruling. As Charles Jackson succinctly put it, the issue was not whether this lapsed dynasty should be reconstituted, but whether it should be reconstituted in favor of "an aged lady tottering on the brink of the grave, who from her age, sex, and Asiatic custom, would be dependent on those around her, or in favour of a minor whose disposition and talents were unknown, and whose minority would itself produce all the evils of an Asiatic Regency" (Jackson 24). Jackson's comments on Raghuji III make it clear that for these Victorian men, women were inimical to good rule: they were a bad influence on men in public life, and as rulers, they were susceptible to bad advisors. So while the British blamed "Asiatic" custom for making Banka Bai dependent on those around her, they did not recognize her as head of the family or as a capable ruler either. Liberal British rule is thus established at the expense of the Rani, who is now represented as unfit to rule, own property, or determine her expenses, and accused of making the indigenous organization of the court suspect and illegitimate.

When Governor-General Dalhousie disposed of the property of the Bhonsle royal family of Nagpur, he also offered the opinion that the provision made for the Ranis was too liberal and more than that allowed to the Ranis of the larger principality of Satara.[9] Dalhousie decided that the Bhonsle property should be at the disposal of the British government, and "in order that it might not be appropriated and squandered by the Ranis," after alloting jewels, furniture and other personal property suitable to their ranks, the rest was to be sold, and the proceeds were to constitute a fund to benefit the Bhonsle family (Rahim 238).

As these measures were put into effect, the Ranis, who had always been compliant, began a series of protests through letters and memoranda, against the annexation of Nagpur, against the denial of their right to adopt, the seizure of their private property, and the public auction of cattle that belonged to the estate of the Raja. In a memorandum to the Governor-General of 17 July 1854, they complained that scant regard had been shown for their feelings after the death of the Raja even though they had not violated any treaties and had always shown loyalty to the British government. In another memorandum, dated 2 September 1854, they complained about the sale of their cattle by public auction. The Ranis disputed every point regarding the distribution of wealth and property. With the Governor-General's approval, it was suggested that the accumulated treasure be used to pay off establishment expenses. Dalhousie's argument was that the treasure was made up of public revenues and did not belong to the Raja. The Ranis claimed that the treasure came from the personal property of the Raja. In his long description of the degeneracy and ineffectiveness of the young Raghuji, Jackson points to one vice more heinous than the rest: "The choicest amusement of the Rajah is an auction sale, when some unfortunate widow is ruled not to be entitled to her husband's estate, or when some public defaulter is found to have made away with revenue collections, just equal to the sum he paid five or six years before his situation of revenue collector to the Rajah" (Jackson 29). Jackson does not seem to note the glaring irony that this is precisely the charge leveled by the widows of Nagpur against the British government. Despite the obvious social and economic disparity between a "poor widow" and the widow of a princely family, the Ranis represented themselves as defenseless and the special responsibility of the state, using rhetoric similar to Jackson's to emphasize the justice of their claims.

In the ensuing drama, the Ranis pledged undying loyalty to the British government but also waged a war of protest against the takeover of their property. Banka Bai threatened to burn down the palace if anything was removed from it, and the harassed Resident reported more than once that the Ranis were obstructing the reorganization of government. Matters came to a head when a protégé of the British was beaten up in the palace, leading to disturbances in the city. A military force was called out, and the Ranis were forbidden to meet friends or advisors of the late Raja. They alleged that a military force carried away jewels of the family worth two million pounds sterling. A European officer took up residence in the palace in order to suitably awe servants loyal to the Ranis. Dalhousie felt convinced that the insurrection had been organized by Banka Bai and communicated his displeasure to the Ranis through the Resident, who was enjoined to "show courtesy and forbearance which were due to their rank, sex and changed condition," but to take recourse to "stringent and coercive measures" if they opposed him, and to disregard "the petulance and vexatious opposition the Ranis may offer" (qtd. in Rahim 243).

Giving up angry protests and appeals to the loyalty and political obligations of the Company, the Ranis decided to seek legal redress from the Board of Control and British Parliament. Their wakils canvassed for support among sympathetic members of British Parliament and were given assurances that the case of the Ranis and the cruelties that the Company inflicted on them would be taken up soon. In a memorial submitted to the court in December 1855, the lawyers asked for restitution of property and jewels belonging to the Ranis. They also maintained that they had a right to appeal to the Court as British subjects. Although Dalhousie's response to Banka Bai's letters reminded her that she was not a representative of the Bhonsle family, he added that "you will consider me as ever anxious to hear of your good health, and continue to gratify me from time to time with account of the same," thereby preserving the elaborate civility with which he and the Ranis were waging this serious political battle (qtd. in Rahim 249). Dalhousie expressed his annoyance at the deputation of wakils sent to England and forced the Ranis to recall them. The Ranis also sent a diplomatic mission to Nepal requesting the British Resident there (who had earlier been posted in Nagpur) to intervene and ease the hostility between them and the Governor-General. Suspicious of their intentions, Dalhousie informed them that they "have no right whatever to communicate with native courts" (qtd. in Rahim 251). The Ranis ultimately lost the battle of wills with the Governor-General, who dismissed their lawyers and imprisoned all the old advisors of the king who were suspected of anti-British activities.

SAMBALPUR

In the political jostling for power in Sambalpur in Western India, the Company directly and aggressively made the case that the Ranis were incapable of holding public office by invoking a suspicion of women in power, their advisors, and their predeliction for rule by whim rather than through "law." While the three other Ranis of the deceased king of Sambalpur remained compliant, the strategy of the eldest Rani was to actively resist the political plans of the Company. When Raja Narayan Singh died heirless in 1849, the title to the throne fell vacant as no immediate family member came forward to claim it. In the uncertainty and turmoil that followed the death of the Raja, the Rani assumed the management of the state. The British Agent Crawfurd reported that immediately after the death of her husband, the Rani placed his turban on her head to show that she had assumed his rights and authority (Rahim 75). Refusing to comply with British colonial agendas, the Rani demanded her rights in a memorial to the Deputy Governor of Bengal, saying that "there were certain usages according to which her husband left instruction to the effect that the eldest Rani be allowed to succeed to the vacant throne after his death, provided she conformed to the wishes and intentions of the government" (Rahim 73).

Sambalpur had been dependent on the turns of Company policy once it had been ceded by the Raja of Nagpur to the Company by the Treaty of Deogaon in 1803. The Company sporadically maintained direct control of the territory but kept in place a figurehead at other times. Ousley, the British Agent, claimed that the gradual takeover of the state would be accomplished with the consent of the Raja. He submitted a detailed report on the condition of the state in 1842 and recommended the annexation of Sambalpur by the British. In his report he outlined the strategic and economic gains likely to accrue to the British by such a move. In contrast to the earlier view that the state would be a liability to manage, Ousley pointed to the richness of the soil and the industry of its people. However, the plan did not find favor with the British high-command, which was more interested in accommodating the wishes of the Raja. Ousley visited Sambalpur in 1847–48 and explained to the Raja the plan of introducing British administration by gradual steps into the state. He was of the opinion that the Raja freely gave his approval to this plan.

After the death of the Raja and in a manner typical of such annexations, records of that period ascribe the failure of the Rani as a ruler to deficiencies in her character. Given the larger socioeconomic causes for unrest in the state, the Rani can hardly be blamed for it. The British Agent Crawfurd alleged that "having taken possession of her husband's personal property, she was secretly plotting with the help of wicked men, in order to regain management of the affairs of the state" (Rahim 75). What follows upon this allegation were further rumors about the Rani's incitement of popular rebellion. She was said to be provoking disturbances that would spread throughout the country if the British government did not find a successor to the throne. Crawfurd observed that "the eldest Rani was notoriously fond of power and was addicted to intrigue" (Rahim 75). It was not difficult for the Resident to "persuade" the Rani that she should leave Sambalpur and go to live in Cuttack on a pension. There were three other widows of the Raja, one of whom had a ten-year-old daughter. While none of these surviving relatives of the Raja were considered an immediate threat, Crawfurd thought that they could become "the subject of intrigue and disturbance if they were allowed to remain at Sambalpur" (Rahim 76). They were therefore dispatched, apparently with their consent, to their native places or to some holy place.

It was tactically important for the British to send the Ranis into retirement with a pension, provide for their daughters, and thus ensure that all claims to the throne were permanently scuttled. In order to accomplish this, the British decided to avail themselves of the services of an old friend of the Raja's family, Tribuhan Singh Deo, a strategy that carried out political machinations through domestic means. Deo was responsible for persuading the Ranis to retire, and taking care of the provisions for them. For this he was rewarded by the British with a pair of shawls for his loyalty to them. However, once the eldest Rani of Sambalpur was given her pension, she did not rest easy in her retirement but presented a petition to the Deputy Governor of Bengal making four requests: first, that there be a successor to the vacant throne (she was willing to conform to the wishes of the British government); second, that failing the first, a suitable settlement be made with her; third, that she be given an appropriate pension and permission to live in Sambalpur; and finally, that her own property be restored to her, as also the property of her husband, of which, according to Hindu law and custom, she alone was the proprietor. Most of her requests were rejected, the state of Sambalpur was annexed, and a British officer was appointed to look after its administration.[10] Appointing a successor to the king was an undesirable step, not only because there were no worthy contenders to the throne, but also because the security and efficient running of the state were at stake. The point, therefore, is that given this peculiar political situation of a childless widow without heirs, the Rani's demand for her own property could become a dangerous political claim. The question of succession blurred the distinction between a personal law and state law as one impinged on the other. Unlike the British government, the Rani saw herself as a possible successor or regent. This self-perception defined her as an independent, sovereign ruler and threatened the British idea of a governable woman and subject.

THE RANI OF JHANSI

I now return to the most spectacular example of a revolt by a widowed Rani against British authority in the story of the Rani of Jhansi. For the British, her assumption of the throne raised questions about a woman assuming political power, her loyalty as a subsidiary of the British, and her customary right to adopt a son. Literary representations of the Rani have been obsessed with her role as the most visible opponent of British rule. In her discussion of a sympathetic contemporary account of the Rani, in John Lang's *Wanderings in India and Other Sketches of Life in Hindostan* (1861), Maria Jerinic points out that Lang's sympathy for the "Ranee" is more as a woman, a private individual, than as a ruler. He portrays her as "the wronged wife of a loyal British subject" rather than a ruler deprived of a state in her own right (Jerinic 129). Jerinic sees this Victorian inability to accept rule by women as legitimate as ultimately a deflection of similar problems with the rule of Queen Victoria. Jerinic notes that in other historical accounts of the Mutiny, contemporary British commentators Walter Erskine and Charles Ball had difficulty giving the Rani of Jhansi the title of "queen" because in claiming political power "the Rani has overstepped her boundaries as a native woman . . . only Victoria, a white woman sovereign, has the right to use this appellation" (Jerinic 128). Female political power created anxiety and fear in most British colonials, who saw it as a threat to empire and nation. Residents and other officials of the East India Company viewed good rule as inevitably masculine while they were suspicious of female influence of any kind.

The final actions of the Rani of Jhansi provide a dramatic instance of the failure of the romance of empire. She refuses to be domesticated into a good subject and pensioner of the British empire and rides into battle against British forces. It is significant, however, that before she decides to go to war, her letters to the British government use terms of negotiation similar to the other Ranis. She emphasizes the written and unwritten contract between the Company and the state of Jhansi when she points to the "favour and protection" of "a mighty power" that has been extended to Jhansi and "uniform and faithful attachment" of her late husband to the British government (Fisher, "Politics" 253).[11] Her letters give a detailed description of the process by which her late husband adopted a son and successor just before he died. The Rani quotes the precedent of other native states which were allowed to adopt sons as successors by the Paramount power. She concludes one of her letters to the Marquis of Dalhousie by listing other central Indian states in which a widow was allowed to adopt a successor to the throne. She reiterates once again "the integrity and justice of the British government" (Fisher, "Politics" 258) and hopes that they would allow her to do the same. A third letter in this series from the Rani to Lord Dalhousie strikes a truly despairing note when she writes:

> . . . if Jhansie is to be absorbed during your Lordship's administration, the five thousand rusty swords worn by the people called its Army and its fifty pieces of harmless ordnance . . . will be delivered over to your Lordship's Agent without any demonstration save that of sorrow—that valuable services should be requited by the confiscation of a puny Kingdom or Raj; which has ever been faithful to the paramount power. (Fisher, "Politics" 259)

The language of this letter keeps intact the civility and docility that is a feature of these exchanges. The Rani puts herself at the mercy of the British government and dutifully follows the script of obedient subject. However, as the conflict escalates, the Rani puts pressure on precisely those points that were most likely to undermine the British sense of themselves as benevolent. She restates the "gross violation and negation of the Treaties of the Government of India . . . and if persisted in they must involve gross violation and negation of British faith and honour" (qtd. in Lebra-Chapman 38). She warns the British of resentment caused among native princes by their hostile actions, and finally, she comments on her own distress at the reduction of her "authority, rank and affluence" and her state of "subjection, dishonor and poverty" (qtd. in Lebra-Chapman 38). The Rani emphasizes that not only are the British involved in dishonorable dealings with a widow whom they do not protect, but that they are responsible for having impoverished her. She makes the further unpalatable point that she has been a capable ruler of Jhansi and that her competence as a ruler has been willfully ignored. She also underscores the fact that she would have been the legal heir of her husband even if he had not left a will. This claim by the Rani points to the anomalous position of widows whose adopted sons and heirs were very young, which meant that the Ranis could rule as regents even if traditional interpretations of customary law disallowed women from becoming direct inheritors of the estates of their husbands. In the Rani's case, the usual British suspicion of the competence of women rulers could not be substantiated, making their imperial intentions in annexing Jhansi even more transparent. The Rani's decision to ride out into battle against British forces is the logical next step in her rebellion, and it exposes the failure of the romance in which she was to play the compliant daughter.

All contemporary and subsequent versions of her death emphasize her heroism. General Rose, the leader of the British forces, called her "the best and the bravest of the rebel leaders," and Charles Ball, another contemporary British observer, called her "an extraordinary female" who shared all the dangers of the struggle when she was struck down.[12] The prominence of the Rani of Jhansi in accounts of the Mutiny can be further ascribed to the fact that she "challenged and disturbed all pronouncements about the natural sexual, racial, and military superiority of British men" (Paxton, *Writing* 142). In late-nineteenth-century British colonial romances, the Rani assumes the burden of representing sexual and political perfidy, Oriental deceit, and the eroticized racial other. Yet despite these strategies of containment, romance writers represent that Rani as a powerful figure who disrupts gender hierarchies, becoming a historical anomaly with which the narrative structure of romances cannot grapple (Paxton, *Writing* 163). In this extended study of the place of Ranis in the British imagination, I argue that the Rani of Jhansi was not anomalous, and that the disturbing questions about hierarchies of gender that she raised by her final act of riding into battle against the

British were raised in other protests by royal widows throughout the nineteenth century.

The romance narrative of liberal colonial rule assumes the consent of the governed. British Residents and the Company were particularly concerned that the subject population and the Ranis recognize the superiority of British rule and obediently accede to it, thereby also becoming educated subjects of the empire. The protests by the Ranis not only give the lie to this liberal fantasy, but also posit an alternative concept of women's status within Hindu and "despotic" monarchial systems. Unlike the Victorian administrators of the Company, the Ranis thought of themselves as rulers, owners of property, prominent in the performance of a customary religious and social duty such as the adoption of a son. In inscribing a history of protest by the widow queens, I rewrite the seamless narrative of British liberal rule. I show the conflict between the Victorian perceptions of separate sphere ideology and different upper-class Indian forms of patriarchy. In the fissure between the two lay the possibility of political protest, which found its most spectacular proponent in the Rani of Jhansi.

CHAPTER FOUR

Educating Seeta

Philip Meadows Taylor's Romances of Empire

In my previous chapter, I discuss how the political conditions of indirect rule, leading to the vexed relationship between the British Resident and the queens of Indian states, create domestic drama. I develop this argument further by reading a record of political conflict between a British Resident and an Indian queen together with his literary fantasy about an interracial marriage. The romantic representation of the Indian woman is a recurring motif in the works of Philip Meadows Taylor (1808–1876), especially in his novel *Seeta* (1872), which represents the education of its eponymous heroine as an ideal colonial subject, creating an elaborate allegory of benevolent government and exposing the limits of its liberal ideology. I show how Seeta is shaped by the ideological premises of the good colonizer and benevolent Orientalist. This becomes evident when the novel is read in conjunction with Taylor's memoir, *Story of My Life*,[1] and his letters to his cousin Henry Reeve which record his political struggle with the Rani of Shorapur.[2]

I argue that Taylor refigures his partially successful imposition of paternal and colonial authority on the queen of Shorapur in the idealized and romantic tropes of the fictional world of Seeta. He rewrites the refractory historical narrative of the resistant queen as an interracial romance, in which the Indian woman in the domestic space becomes an educable and willing native subject. As I show in my previous chapter, in such conflicts between the British Resident and the widowed queens of native states, the gendered division of spaces into public and domestic, and the relation of sexual morality to the exercise of public power, call forth the disciplinary impulses of patriarchal colonial authority. These impulses are realized in the fictional world of Taylor's *Seeta*, where the fictional wife is transformed into an eager and receptive student. Taylor's historical writing, on the other hand, casts the Rani of Shorapur as a disobedient subject who resists her political lessons. And, as I point out in my reading of other interracial romances, here too, the instability of the romantic narrative and its ambiguous closure points as much to the failure of benevolent colonialism as to its desired ends.

Taylor is one of the most prolific of those nineteenth-century British administrators who lived, worked, and authored literary works in India. He inaugurated a genre of writing about India of which Rudyard Kipling became the most famous exponent. These texts combined strains of historical, romantic, adventure, and domestic Victorian fiction with the difference that Indian scenes and characters were allowed a representational scope which the Victorian novel did not allow. Most of Taylor's writings present romantic versions of Indian subjects and Indian history in a style reminiscent of Walter Scott. *Tipoo Sultaun: A Tale of the Mysore War* (1840), *Tara: a Mahratta Tale* (1863), *Ralph Darnell* (1865), *A Noble Queen: A Romance of Indian History* (1878), and *Seeta* all present idealized portraits of Indians in the midst of historical events. *Seeta* narrates the events of the Revolt of 1857, and unlike most other fiction of the period, endows the rebellious—and ultimately irredeemable—Indian outlaws with a touch of anti-imperial heroism. The weight of Taylor's idealistic representation of Indians, however, is borne by the heroine of the novel which encodes within the love and marriage plot of sentimental fiction a fable about successful colonial governance.

Taylor is best known for *Confessions of a Thug* (1833), a sensational account of the life of a 'thug' who made his living by strangling and robbing travelers. In this novel, Ameer Ali, a captured Thug, recounts to a British police official the horrifying story of several gruesome murders and robberies committed by him. The campaign against Thugs in early-nineteenth-century India was directed against what the British perceived as barbarous Hindu customs practiced by a criminal tribe (the Thugs were devotees of Hindu goddess Kali). Colonel Sleeman earned most of the accolades for the success of his anti-Thugi campaign, but it is less well-known that Philip Meadows Taylor also contributed to the elimination of Thugi. Although the confessions of Ameer Ali are placed within and judged by the framework of rational British law, there are moments of sympathy with the protagonist who is at different times a family man mourning the loss of his son, a swaggering charmer who elicits the fleeting admiration of the listening British officer, and a story teller who presents the rich texture of a polyglot and lively indigenous culture.³ Taylor's deep involvement with colonial India is evident in his strong and complex portrayal of Indian criminals and outlaws in his later fiction too. His own experience in India and the Indian origin and location of his writings were surely responsible for the daringly sympathetic depiction of interracial love leading to marriage between a British official and a young Indian widow in *Seeta*.⁴ There are very few contemporary Anglo-Indian literary works that not only make interracial marriage their central theme, but also present it as a romantic and ideal possibility.

In my analysis of Philip Meadows Taylor's autobiographical writings, fictional accounts, and records of political negotiations I propose not only that these writings constitute a continuous archive detailing the minutiae of the establishment of colonial authority, but also that the biographical and anecdotal have a special status as colonial documents, providing a web of discursive interconnections between the historical, the literary, and the political. In emphasizing the importance of Taylor's personal history, however, I would like to distinguish my approach from histories of empire that foreground the private lives of colonial administrators. For example, in his history of the British empire, Ronald Hyam writes that the renewed interest in biography has made it possible to write a social history of empire in which the private lives of administrators, jurists, and political figures are accorded as much importance as facts about the economic and political life of both the colonizing and the subject people. Hyam describes the personal lives of the men and women who ruled as a source of strength and sustenance for them and hence a major influence on their public life. He suggests further that nineteenth-century empires were a consequence of the sublimation of sexual energy (Hyam, *Empire and Sexuality* 1990). While I agree with Hyam that attention to colonial biographies is indispensable to a writing of the social history of empire, I emphasize the study of a social and political formation of a colonial ruling class rather than the foibles and glories of a group of people and how they sought their strengths in a variety of personal relationships.

Taylor's life and work show a rich confluence of colonial ideology, Orientalist history, and literary imagination influenced by nineteenth-century English fiction. He came to India to seek his fortune as an independent adventurer and found employment neither with the Crown nor with the East India Company. Instead, he set out for Bombay at a very young age to seek his fortune as an apprentice. The business failed, but he was fortunate to find the patronage of a family friend, which led him to his first stable job in the army of the Nizam[5] of Hyderabad. However, this meant a much lower start in life than most employees of the East India Company as well as being without the privilege and security attached to such employment. Taylor had a successful career despite the fact that his position was dependent on the vagaries of British relations with Indian states. In 1841, he became Political Agent in Shorapur, a feudatory state under the Nizam, and worked for social and administrative reforms in the area under his jurisdiction. Since he was not a direct employee of the Company, Taylor felt free to criticize its policies and maintain a certain freedom from official injunction in his personal life.

He enjoyed a mixed social life in Hyderabad which was facilitated by a culturally syncretic, liberal society, more tolerant of the mixing of races and cultures than elsewhere in India. Many of the officers of the Nizam's army included the offspring of mixed marriages between Europeans and Indian women. Taylor enjoyed the rich indigenous culture at the Nizam's court and was quite comfortable smoking a hookah in Indian dress. At the house of his friend William Palmer, a prominent banker, Taylor met "the most intelligent members of Hyderabad society, both native and European, and the pleasant gatherings . . . were a great relief from the state and formality of the Residency" (*Story* 37). Palmer's father had been Military Secretary to Governor-General Warren Hastings, and had married a Muslim woman from the princely family of the northern state of Oudh. This same Begum of Oudh lived with William Palmer Jr. and is remembered by Taylor as a respected member of the household. When in 1832 Taylor married Palmer's daughter Mary, he entered a mixed marriage with a woman whose paternal grandmother was Indian. In world view and sensibility, Taylor thus belonged to that period in the eighteenth century when such unions between prominent Englishmen and Indian women were quite common. (I discuss this at length in my study of the life of William Linneaus Gardner in chapter 1.)

Rather anomalously for a nineteenth-century colonial ideologue, Taylor was cast in the mold of the good Orientalists of the eighteenth century.[6] In true Orientalist spirit, he was proficient in the local languages and applied himself to the study of local customs. Like the Orientalists of an earlier era, he believed in India's past glory and rich tradition, and its current state of decay. In constructions of classical Orientalism, India's glorious Hindu past put it on a par with contemporary Western civilization, but its present degeneration by no means allowed that equivalence. In fact, Taylor had to confront the grim reality of empty state coffers, political intrigue, and a beleaguered ruling class whose alliance with the British was unreliable.

When he became Political Agent of Shorapur in 1841, he found that his official duties were intertwined with his relationship to the recalcitrant queen of that state. Taylor's letters to Henry Reeve show that his dealings with the Rani greatly preoccupied him. She seems embroiled in almost every decision related to the business of the state, particularly the reorganization of revenue and police administration. Her unwillingness to give up control of the state prompts Taylor to undertake strong measures to contain her while still retaining a firm belief in his benevolence. Over the course of Taylor's administration, the Rani is coerced into becoming an obedient ally of the British. Taylor establishes his authority not only through his administrative functions, but also through the political lessons that he teaches the Rani. These lessons are punitive reminders that in seeking political power, she has offended traditional proprieties of gender, violated her role as an upper-class woman confined to the domestic sphere, and refused the patronage that she should have gratefully accepted.

Taylor and the Rani of Shorapur

Taylor's memoir presents a studied, formal account of his dealings with the obdurate Rani of Shorapur. His letters, though they describe the same historical events, are more strongly worded, unrestrained expressions of anger and exasperation at the political debacles and local intrigues she instigates. The Rani's public role as head of the state is particularly significant in light of the fact that women of ruling families in Indian states could be politically active only as regents of male heirs. While in most cases the Company deprived them of this right by using doctrine of lapse, the case of Shorapur was slightly different in that the British government kept the ruling family as nominal head of the state while placing revenue administration, maintenance of a police force, and diplomatic relations in the hands of a British representative. Taylor informs us that this Rani, the deceased king's senior queen, had taken a "menial" as her paramour, seized control of the state, and become regent for her eight-year-old son. In his memoir, Taylor describes her as "a woman of much energy and cleverness but dissolute to a degree—

in fact a very Messalina" (*Story* 120),[7] making a connection between sexual and political unscrupulousness which dominates his account of the Rani. In Taylor's account, the Rani is rebellious, fractious, intractable, abject, and docile by turns, justifying his unambiguous exercise of power. His negotiations with her, which mostly involved the extraction of revenue, required a firm, even ruthless attitude, while as an officer in the Nizam's army he was called upon to mediate between the Nizam, the British, and the Rani.

Taylor's letters show that his diplomatic skills were severely tested when he tried to hold the Rani to her promise of paying revenue to the Nizam. When the British Resident asks Taylor to intercede in this matter, he speaks to her followers separately, before she has time to muster them. Determined and uncompromising, Taylor puts three propositions before her which sound more like injunctions to surrender all her power: she must hand over all her accounts and the seal of office, and give up her armed men. Instead of relying on her promises as his predecessor had done, Taylor sends for her followers one by one and forces them to swear allegiance to the Nizam and the British. Taylor notes with relish the punitive, sadistic force behind his interaction with the renegade queen: "one by one the leaders were sent, and I had to screw them out of her, like drops of blood but I got all" (*Letters* 87).

The Rani includes Taylor in her domestic circle, seemingly accepting his authority, but ultimately plots against him and promotes general unrest in the state. At their first meeting, Taylor breaks to her the news that Pid Naik, the deceased king's oldest brother, will be made king, and her son the next heir, but that she can no longer be regent. Although she is upset by this news, and Taylor unrelenting in his demand for the revenue, he reports that their meeting was quite cordial: "for a time she spoke very pleasantly, and the little Rajah had, of his own accord, come to me, and was sitting in my lap. 'See,' said the Ranee, 'my son has gone to you, as he never did to his father, and now you must be father to us all'" (*Story* 125). In saying this, the Rani may be repeating a well-known designation of the Company as "father-mother." However, this paternal designation of the real economic and political power assumed by the Company is also a recognition that Taylor has replaced the child's natural father as provider and protector. Above all, by addressing Taylor in familial terms, the Rani hopes from him not an uncompromising stance as an administrator, but instead his paternal indulgence towards her. The Rani appeals to familial obligation not for the romantic resolution of political conflict but to make political capital of the domestic situation.

Conversely, Taylor describes her political machinations and protests against the imposition of British rule as irrational feminine outbursts. While Taylor considers himself an embodiment of rational law and authority, the Rani, he says, "would not listen to any reason at all in regard to the money she herself had promised" (*Letters* 94). The Rani's family, angered by her taking a low-caste lover, recommend to Taylor that the deceased king's older brother be made king. Taylor places the Rani's advisor, popularly perceived to be her paramour, under surveillance in his camp. The Rani's attempt to negotiate with Taylor as an equal does not work, nor is she allowed to have her way in any matter relating to the state. On learning that she is getting together an armed militia to attack his camp and free her lover, Taylor dispatches the man to another place out of her reach. Taylor reports that the Rani responded by trying to incite rebellion against him:

> Great was the indignation and consternation of the Lady in the morning. She beat her head, and, as it was reported to me, knocked it against the wall, roared and cried, and then, in a violent passion, rushed into the outer court of her palace, and called upon all good men and true to help her get Chun Basappa back again. This was the crisis I expected, and upon it would turn everything, hostile and peaceable. But nobody stirred. . . . Well my Lady then was down on her marrow-bones for a few days, and my humble servant. (*Story* 132)

Describing her rage at her inability to defeat him by force, Taylor revels in the sardonic inversion of the chivalrous relation by which "My Lady" becomes his "humble servant" rather than the other way round. Having "squeezed" her allies out of her like "drops of blood," he now rejoices that she is "down on her marrow bones." Sending for troops to stand by in case of trouble, Taylor demands payment from her in terms of disciplinary punishment: "I shall give the lady another sad blow tomorrow, as, if she does not give the money or account for it, all her Jagheer (land given to members of a ruling family for maintenance) villages are to be occupied by parties of Cavalry, whom I have all ready to slip" (*Letters* 95). Having failed to use force against him, the Rani becomes placatory, sending him "a series of sorrowful letters," and many gifts (*Letters* 95). Taylor is uncompromising in his demand for the one lakh (one hundred thousand) rupees she owes the British government. The Rani, resorting to her domestic role once again, visits Taylor with her son and is promptly granted forgiveness. While Taylor narrates this episode as another instance of his righteous triumph over the manipulative Rani, considering the Rani's abjection as a lesson taught in political subservience and a reinforcement of her dependent and domestic position, she seeks the security of her 'proper sphere' only until she can make her next political move.

Almost a month after this incident, Taylor has another confrontation with the Rani, who has been trying to mobilize forces against British rule: "My troublesome Ranee came the other day and threw herself at my feet whether I would or no, and we had the quarrel out. She was very penitent and is now my particular friend; she sees what a fool she has been plainly enough, and having burnt her fingers will meddle no more with politics" (*Letters* 98). This uneasy peace is disturbed yet again in September of that year, when Taylor learns that a force of five hundred men has been secretly prepared to invade Shorapur. Taylor's exasperation at the new disturbances in the state is expressed as a general suspicion of the women of ruling families: "The person at the bottom of it is the Ranee, and one of her paramours is very busy also. . . . The Ranee is a shameless devil, and these people of hers will one day or other get her into such a mess, that she will be sent off to Benaras or some other holy place where she can amuse herself with fat Brahmins ad lib. These Ranees are everywhere the same, Lahore, Gwalior, Kolapoor, Indore, not a shade of difference except what results from differences in shamelessness" (*Letters* 199). The "shameless" Ranis commit not only a breach of decorum but also encroach on public and political spaces inappropriate for women. It is no coincidence that many of the Ranis that Taylor mentions earned the ire of their families and the British government both for their 'immorality' and for inciting political rebellion, or that British administrators in other Indian states also read a breach of the decorum of domesticity on the part of women rulers as an act of political rebellion.

The invention of the good colonizer as surrogate parent is premised on the Rani's 'wickedness' and her failure as mother and domestic angel. Perceiving the Rani as a neglectful mother turns Taylor from a political antagonist into an angry father or disapproving husband. The negotiations between the Rani and Taylor involving the education of her son and heir to the throne take on the aspect of a domestic quarrel. Taylor takes charge of the education of the young Raja, which for him means turning the Raja into an ally of the British government. From him, the Raja learns a growing suspicion of his discredited mother, and learns also to address Taylor as "appa" or father. The prodigal Rani fails to "learn" any form of obedience and repeats political and domestic maneuvers till the day she dies. She weeps tears of gratitude when Taylor ceremonially installs the young prince on the throne, then incites her son to rebel against the British. When she falls ill, she summons Taylor to her bedside, and roundly curses her son. The immediate cause of her anguish is a prophecy that her son would die in his twenty-fourth year: "All that concerns that base-born boy is bad! Why did his father die? Why did I not strangle him with my own hands rather than let a wretch like that live to be the ruin of the state? . . . I am dying myself, and you English have made him secure to glory in my death!" (*Story* 228). These ravings of a sick woman become supplicatory when she begs Taylor to stay with her son until the day of his death and bequeaths the state to Taylor and his children. She ends by asserting the familial terms of their relationship once again : "O Taylor Sahib! you have been a father and mother to me, and I have often used you very ill. I am a wicked woman, and deserve punishment . . . " (*Story* 229). The Rani's abasement constructs Taylor's benevolence as familial in nature, while at the same time pointing to the latent sadism in the idea of the benevolent colonizer. Her final appeal to Taylor's authority exposes the fiction of benevolent authority that is the basis of the romance of empire. For Taylor, this satisfying narrative closure is achieved only with the death of the Rani and her final subjection to his authority.

Seeta

Taylor's fictional interracial romance, *Seeta*, sets out to provide an ideal version of the family romance, and stands as a counterpoint to the turbulent narrative of the Rani of Shorapur in which political and domestic amicability are only partially achieved. In this romance, the Indian woman gives moral legitimacy to colonial rule when her desires lead her into an English officer's life and home, there to exemplify not only the liberal intermixing of different races and cultures, but also the justice and goodness of British rule. *Seeta* can be read, then, as a fictional rewriting of the place of the native woman in the colonial imaginary. If the coercive mechanisms of the colonial state slowly and only imperfectly domesticate the Rani, the novel completes that domestication of the woman as colonial subject in the figure of Seeta.

Early in the novel, Seeta is widowed when a vicious, greedy Brahmin, Azrael Pande, and his gang of thugs attack and rob her house, killing her husband in the process.[8] The naming of the novel's archvillain suggests that Taylor reached deep into his mythological repertoire and ignored verisimilitude, which only underscores the 'romantic,' fictional nature of *Seeta* even though it incorporates actual historical events. Azrael is the formidable and ruthless angel of death in Christian, Jewish, and Islamic literature. It is unlikely that Pande, a Brahmin, would have a first name that came from the literature of the Abrahamic religions. In keeping with Taylor's ambivalent relationship with his anti-heroes, Azrael is both admired and feared in all three religious traditions. Taylor neatly ranges his heroes against villains who combine vendetta with political unrest. His colonial spaces are thus partitioned into the domestic, which encloses the idealized female colonial subject and forms the locus of the sentimental plot, and the wild, threatening caves and fields which become masculine spaces occupied by bandits who exist outside and in opposition to the economy of English law and governance.

Most importantly for my purposes here, the novel is also an interracial love story: Seeta, a young widow, marries Cyril Brandon, the English collector of Noorpor. Her beauty and learning attract not only the notice of the Englishman, but also the lust of the cruel bandit chief Azrael Pande who makes several attempts to kidnap her, which are foiled each time by the vigilance of the Englishman and his loyal followers. The novel becomes a battle to possess Seeta, who gives herself up to being Cyril's devoted and grateful wife while trying at the same time to "preserve her caste" by religiously performing the rituals required of her. At the end, Seeta proves her loyalty by throwing herself in front of Cyril to save him from a murderous attack by Azrael Pande. She is killed in the melee, leaving her husband free to marry an Englishwoman of the appropriate class.

The figure of the widow as the vehicle for the articulation of British imperial ideology is particularly significant given her large presence in the debates about social reform which were used to justify British intervention in Indian social and cultural affairs. Taylor's widow is a romantic heroine acting on her own behalf rather than a traditional widow, confined by the boundaries of the home and unavailable for tutelage or romance. While Seeta is passively acted upon at first, she is later endowed with an active will and a desire to learn, which makes her not only an Orientalist's delight, but also unusually receptive to Cyril. She is not an untutored savage but a woman of learning and accomplishment, and therefore more desirable as "an ornament"[9] in Cyril's house. Following Orientalist constructions of India's rich heritage and ancient civilization that envisioned a "golden age" of Hindu civilization, in which women were accorded a high place in society,

Taylor's Seeta moves around freely and unveiled, has been taught to read, has studied the Indian classics, and even appears in court to give testimony.

In the opening pages of the novel, Seeta is a docile, timid, loving wife who fears for her husband's well-being. She is also a young mother devoted to her child and the household. But though she is rumored to be beautiful and the object of male desire, the author's gaze does not turn to her physical attributes until she appears in court before the district magistrate, Cyril Brandon. This is particularly significant given that the novel's moral universe revolves around the nobility of the Englishman's desire for Seeta and her reciprocal love for him, which is set against Azrael Pande's lawless and unrequited passion for her. Cyril gives his desire moral legitimacy by elevating it into a purer desire to marry Seeta, while Azrael's wild fantasies about enslaving her incriminate him morally and politically. Yet Cyril too is attracted by Seeta's helplessness, which places him in the position of her savior and makes her potentially his dependent. As he watches her giving testimony in his court, he notes that:

> The large dewy eyes were soft and pleading, but not irresolute, and the girl was quite calm. Seeta had dressed herself in a rich silk saree of a green colour, shot through with crimson, which had heavy borders and ends of gold thread, and the end which she passed over her head, fell on her right arm and contrasted vividly with its fair colour and rounded outline. If her features were not exactly regular, they were very sweet and full of expression; her eyes were large and soft, of that clear dark brown which, like a dog's is always so loving and true. If the mouth were a shade too full for exact symmetry, it was mobile and expressive, and the curves of the upper lip constantly varied. (61)

Taylor's intense concentration on making Seeta the embodiment of soft, gentle, suppliant womanhood prompts the absurd exaggeration of the dog-like eyes, always loving and true. By making Seeta like "a Titian picture," her skin "a rich golden olive, with bright carnation tint rising under the skin" (61), he accommodates her within a European ideal, and where she falls short of that ideal in shape and form, she makes up for it in sentiment and emotion. Even though Brandon could not see her face, her "small graceful head, the rounded arm, the tiny foot, the graceful movement of the neck, and her springy lithe step as she had entered the tent, assured him that it could not be less beautiful than the face" (61). It is also significant that Taylor shows Seeta in a white sari at the time of the robbery—traditionally a color worn by widows—and shows her clad in rich silks after she has been widowed, quite contrary to the norms of the orthodox community of which Seeta is a part. This public appearance of a widow in resplendent garb marks her as exceptional and leaves a lasting impression on Cyril's mind.

Seeta and Cyril experience the higher satisfactions of romantic love as they get better acquainted through their shared interest in classical Sanskrit literature. Seeta's readings to Cyril from the epic *Mahabharat*[10] serves as the conduit for ennobling sentiment, intellectual curiosity, and romantic passion. Cyril remembers his own reading of this epic, which narrates, among others, the story of the undying devotion of a Hindu wife for her husband, whom she follows to the nether world after his death. Being well-read in Indian classic epic, drama, and romantic poetry, Seeta is aware of a literary ideal of love that is impassioned, free, and on a higher plane than duty. An awareness of this love also makes her receptive to English poetry and creates a desire for Cyril's companionship. Romantic love, with its liberal belief in freely given affection, obscures the ideology that constructs subjugation as love. Without the necessary fiction of a free will, Seeta would be no different from the passive Hindu woman imagined by Europeans. In their accounts, as Kumkum Sangari explains in her discussion of the late-eighteenth-century travelogue of Abbe Dubois, chastity and passivity become figures for governability:

> The Hindu woman who played into the larger frames of European mistrust of female sexuality and the stereotype of the licentious Orient, is simultaneously set apart as the soothing exemplum of chastity, a model for Western women to emulate. . . . The passivity ascribed to Hindu men and the egoless subjection ascribed to women under patriarchal dominance are in miniature aspects of the governability of India—two favourable conditions among others for colonial rule. (Sangari 54)

Although Seeta shares the passivity of the Oriental woman, a liberal belief in the willing collusion of the colonial subject requires her to exercise her choice in favor of Cyril. Her governability is thus a consequence of her passivity and her receptivity to a program of education in the arts and literature of England.

In her discussion of the introduction of English literary studies in India, Gauri Viswanathan points out that education acquired a special significance when force gave way to "moral and intellectual suasion" as a strategy to consolidate colonial rule.[11] Debates on the question of formulating an education policy for the natives divided British administrators into the Orientalist and the Anglicist camps. While the Orientalists advocated development of India's vernacular languages and literatures, the Anglicists were strongly supportive of instruction in English language and literature. The teaching of English was meant not only to disseminate the language of progress but also to create a new kind of colonial subject.[12] Seeta exemplifies this Anglicist subject when Taylor describes her tentative acculturation into British social life as an awakening of her intellect. Her aspirations to the pleasures of Western arts and letters include learning English so that she can read "the poetry of England" (184). The sentimental resolution of the marriage between Seeta and Cyril is represented as her growing interest in the music of Mozart, in Cyril's sketches of her—one of which shows her with her arms stretched appealing to British justice—and in English and Italian poets. All the benevolent elements of the Anglo-Indian community join forces to 'educate' Seeta. Cyril informs Mrs Mostyn and Grace, the wife and sister of his friend and colleague Philip Mostyn, that "Seeta is studying English very hard and hopes some day to be able to talk with you easily" (202). They exclaim in wonder at Seeta's growing familiarity with English, and the terms of their social interaction are settled when it becomes clear that she is a worthy disciple. Taylor's Seeta also plays the native collaborator whose knowledge and skills are quietly absorbed into the task of colonial government. Taking on the role of office scribe, she reads out to Cyril passages from vernacular newspapers so that he can translate them into English.

The significance of Seeta's compliant domesticity in affirming colonial authority becomes evident when we consider that outside the domestic lies unmitigated villainy and lawlessness. If Seeta, the colonial woman, stands for the educable native allied with British interest and favor, the lesser or greater shades of evil embodied in the Indian men are represented as their unteachability. As opposed to the private, domestic space of the interior of homes, the open stretches of country they are associated with are dangerous and threatening. Taylor informs us that a Buddhist monastery that was built in the spot known for "its wild beauty and absolute seclusion" (2) has other sinister associations as well: "It was not without cause that this place had earned an evil reputation by night as well as by day. Inside the old Bodhist temple were the ashes of fires, with broken earthen vessels strewed about them; and among these were coarse earthen crucibles in which the booty of many a Pindharee foray, or Dacoity, had been melted down." The "savage" men who live in caves around there live "a hard lawless life" (3).

Unlike his literary ideal Walter Scott, who makes heroes of his highland outlaws, Taylor paints a grisly and horrifying picture of the Indian bandits as marauders, plunderers, lustful and unscrupulous men who are discredited in every way. However, he expresses a residual sympathy with the leader of the group, Azrael Pande, whom he describes in some detail:

> A tall commanding figure, with a great breadth of chest and strength of limb, showing the constant use of athletic exercises. His features were regular, and would have been handsome but for his mouth, which, when he spoke, disclosed jagged irregular teeth; and together with some projection of the lower jaw gave him, when excited, the expression of a wild beast. The coal-black eyes were large, deep-set, and fierce in expression. On his forehead, which was high and smooth, a strange knot of wrinkles would often arise suddenly, and those who knew him best feared him most when these appeared. For a native of India, his complexion might be called fair—a bright olive, which sometimes flushed into dark red. His thick moustache was streaked with grey, and his age might be forty years, while his powerful frame and soldier-like carriage betokened no decay of power in what was evidently the prime of his life. (5)

Taylor's description of Azrael expresses a covert admiration for his strength and martial bearing. Azrael's fair complexion and high and smooth forehead bring him closer to European ideals of male beauty, while his vigorous, strong, and vicious personality is a marked departure from the tradition of depicting Hindu men as effeminate. Governor-general Warren Hastings's description of the Hindu temperament in 1813 expressed a belief shared by many British administrators. He describes Hindus as "gentle, benevolent, more susceptible of gratitude for kindness shown them, than prompted to vengeance for wrongs inflicted, and as exempt from the worst propensities of human passion as any people upon the face of the earth; they are faithful and affectionate in service, and submissive to legal authority; they are superstitious, it is true, but they do not think ill of us for not thinking as they do."[13] In contrast to this, Taylor represents Hindus as aggressive and murderous, a conclusion that he probably bases on his experience of dealing with dacoits and outlaws in his term as Police Commissioner of Hyderabad and one which fits in perfectly with his representation of the ungovernable, unteachable leader of the bandits.[14]

Azrael's active involvement in the Revolt of 1857,[15] also called the

First War of Indian Independence, makes him the type of the uneducable male subject. He becomes the fictional spokesperson for many antagonisms against the British as he exhorts his captive audience, composed of men from the regiment from which he was dismissed when charged with robbery and murder, to join the revolt. Azrael begins his bitter condemnation of the British by accusing them of having turned into "a mean, cheating robber, who farms this great Hind of ours from the Government of England, and robs it of all it can carry away" (147). He lists drain of economic wealth, usurpation of hereditary rights of kingship, and interference with the custom of adoption among the rulers of princely states as instances of the Company's injustice and greed. As he gets more and more impassioned, Azrael's harangue is dominated by resentment caused by the Company's interference in the religious and cultural life of its subjects, specially in relation to social reform for women: "look you, my sons, how hellish are the contrivances to sap the very foundations of Hindoo faith and purity. Now the law is gone forth that Hindoo widows may marry again. . . . Think, any one of you, where your honour would be, if your widow married another man? Where would be the old respect and love which sealed the devotion of its life by holy suttee?" (150). On this issue, Azrael speaks for those conservative sections of Hindu society that resented British initiatives for bringing in laws making Sati illegal. While Taylor faithfully records the reasons for popular discontent and anger against the British as well as the anti-imperial sentiment of Azrael's speech, it is surely no coincidence that the core of Azrael's grand peroration is his defense of the practice of Sati against widow remarriage. This makes him inimical to our heroine, and places him in direct opposition to her savior, the British administrator. Following most historical accounts of he Mutiny, Taylor represents political malcontents, outlaws and criminals, disaffected soldiers, and conservative religious fanatics as allies of the rebels. However, by making all reasons for anti-British feeling the same, he succeeds in presenting it as an uprising of the morally depraved against just and benevolent rule. While he allows a sympathetic airing of social, political, and economic grievances against the British, he also pathologizes these grievances as deficiencies in the moral fiber of the rebels.

The moral and psychological flaws revealed in Azrael's attitude towards Seeta are a part of the same set of failings that make him an ungovernable, lawless subject. His villainy reaches its culmination in his mad desire to capture Seeta and enslave her. While in prison awaiting the execution of his death sentence, he dreams of escape and of making "the proud Seeta . . . his slave—far away in the Eastern lands, she should be his slave till she died. As his mind revelled in her beauty, he raved in the night" (89). Lying hidden in the Nawab's palace, injured and delirious, his grisly physical maiming matches the ravings of his imagination. He is racked by "hideous dreams," his eyes fill with tears and he stretches out his arms and cries out, "Seeta! Seeta! O beloved, come to me! O beloved, give me thy love, as thou hast mine! O lotos feet; I hear the sound of thy softly tinkling anklets! O lithe and swaying form advancing with dainty steps, I would embrace thee!" (300). These ravings taper off into the vindictive fancies of thwarted passion : "Ah! witch, sorceress . . . polluted as thou art, come to me! Seeta, dost thou not hear? Whither wouldst thou fly? Harlot! I will defile thee! I will crush thee! Thou shalt be my slave; and thy paramour Brandon shall not save thee from Azrael Pande!" (300).

Azrael's passion for Seeta makes him Cyril's rival but also his alter ego. Cyril, exorcising his lust for Seeta, or channeling it into the respectable form of marriage, presents a mirror image of the lawless passion of Azrael. Thus, Cyril's victory over himself can be read as an allegory of the nobility and justness of British rule. In the agonistic encounter between Cyril and Azrael, winning Seeta bestows legitimacy on Cyril's desire, which is structurally similar to Azrael's. Early in the novel, Cyril first invokes and then exorcises his dishonorable intentions towards Seeta. As he thinks of the grim possibilities that lie before her as a widow, the desire to make her happy takes the vague form of a liaison with her: "how many as good as he had formed such connections, some for life and others till they married" (115). Taylor describes his decision to proposition her as a moment of weakness prompted by the devil:

> And one night, when he was alone, and his tempter was busy with his soul, he sat down and wrote—wrote such words as he was sure Seeta would read with secret joy and exultation and would not reprove him. But—and I may say it not irreverently—his mind as he read it over, presently rejected what he had written; rejected it as dishonourable and insulting, and he prayed to be delivered from his temptation; and as he cried, "Lord, I am sinking; save me ere I perish!" he tore up the letter into small fragments and burned them. In Seeta's intercourse with him he remembered that he had never detected any trace of levity, and he felt that she believed him, as she had told him once, pure and good. (115)

Cyril holds up as exemplary eighteenth-century alliances between Indian women and employees of the East India Company or senior army officers, which occasionally culminated in marriage. Cyril and his friend Mostyn consider these relationships evidence of the cordial and open interaction between the two races. The elaborate staging of the temptation of Cyril Brandon and the triumphant victory over his baser instincts reinstate bourgeois marriage as the only honorable relation between him and Seeta. Her virtue becomes the touchstone of a civilized, lawful, and just social dispensation, and she gives moral and political legitimacy to British rule by becoming Cyril's wife. The romantic plot depicts this colonial dynamic allegorically. Since official British opinion favored racial and cultural segregation in this period, the fictional invention of interracial love works as a phantasmatic projection of colonial aspirations and native collusion.

Before he can find the plot devices that would neatly bring about narrative closure, however, Taylor's plots clash with and contradict each other, causing serious logical and psychological inconsistencies. The sentimental narrative of the love between Seeta and Cyril is suddenly arrested with the arrival in the Anglo-Indian community of Grace Mostyn, the idealized English woman whose beauty and "the delicate and highly toned colour of her mind" (170) impress Cyril at once. Taylor introduces here a story that is at odds with the interracial romance that has formed the focus of the novel till this point. Almost losing interest in the earlier story, he gives the novel the expected sentimental twist and abandons Seeta to the usual fate of the dark-haired heroine in nineteenth-century fiction. Cyril's growing interest in Grace Mostyn has now to be balanced with his continuing commitment to Seeta. Taylor resolves this authorial dilemma with dismissive remarks that betray his discomfort with the narrative tangle he has created. As Cyril gets more and more involved in the social world of the Mostyns, Taylor remarks, "I am sadly afraid he did not get back [to Seeta] as soon as he could on all occasions. Somehow or another there was always new music to be practiced at the Mostyns, which he could not refuse, and where his welcome seemed to grow warmer every day; and that sweet, fresh face of Grace's to beam with greater pleasure and intelligence as she selected her favourite pieces and sung to him, now without reserve, and with all the skill and abandon of her great musical talents. I am afraid too, that Seeta's English lessons were but slightly attended to, and the sail on the lake often altogether missed" (190).

Seeta's transformation from Orientalist fantasy to narrative superfluity seems so much at odds with the rest of the novel, that I was compelled to seek an explanation for this turn of events outside the narrative itself. Taylor begins with a profoundly conservative Orientalism which posits the absolute difference of cultures but which, as his idealization of Seeta's learning shows, also posits the greatness of highly evolved classical cultures. From there he moves to the liberal ideology of reform and cultural improvement through English education, which, as it leads to a finer sensibility and a modern consciousness, must supplant Indian arts and literature. He finally abandons the educable native so as to reestablish a normative sentimental plotline, the basis of which is a racial and cultural sympathy between a middle-class English man and woman, and which, by excluding Seeta, reestablishes the absolute difference between cultures and people.

It becomes clear in the debates about introducing English to Indians that it had value both as a medium of instruction and as the bearer of a modern sensibility and a scientific mindset. The Orientalist view that this could be grafted onto indigenous languages is expressed in Taylor's portrayal of Seeta. Her learning in traditional Sanskrit literature and her training in Indian music makes her receptive to Western literature, art, and music. Yet halfway through the novel, Taylor's faith in the success of this grafting falters. Seeta can only aspire to rather than achieve an English ideal of learning and artistic accomplishment. She must painstakingly learn to appreciate the music of Mozart and the English language, both of which come easily to Grace Mostyn. Perhaps subconsciously divining this inadequacy, Seeta descends into a state of Gothic fear that Cyril means to abandon her, calling forth protestations of loyalty and commitment from him. Taylor moves from the cultural conservatism of thinking that Seeta could continue to live the life of a good Hindu woman while Cyril participates alone in the social rituals of the expatriate British community, to the belief that after their marriage Seeta could adopt the English language and acquire an appreciation of English culture. He finally returns to a cultural conservatism that cannot envision the social consequences of such grafting in Seeta.

If Taylor's unexplained loss of interest in Seeta's fate can be ascribed to the limits and limitations of his social vision, it can also be ascribed to the lack of literary antecedents which would allow him to work through the consequences of Seeta's possible coming of age in Anglo-Indian society. Both these express the contradictions of liberal colonialism that I have discussed before and that is expressed in these kinds of jarring narrative twists. For instance, the administrative pragmatism which marked education policy in India, and which was accompanied by the fear that educated Indians would soon demand complete independence, is echoed in Cyril's desire to educate Seeta, but also the caution with which he approaches her desire for knowledge. He wants to encourage in her not the absolute freedom of an untrammeled quest, but her gradual transformation into an educated subject. Framed in the proprietary and commanding language of master/husband, he expresses his desire to "direct and restrain, rather than stimulate the passion for knowledge which he saw was awakening in the girl's mind" (153). He reads to her passages from Italian and English poets but thinks, "she is mine for life, . . . and there is time enough to bring out all these strange graces and mould them into form and exercise. I must be careful not to excite her too much" (153). Seeta's education has to stay within the strict bounds that would make her subsidiary to the interests of colonial governance because in the hope of a growing proficiency in English lay also the hope of upward mobility for the Indian subjects. Seeta, proficient in western arts and letters, would otherwise make the kinds of narrative demands that Taylor cannot concede to her. Is Seeta's growing familiarity with the English language arrested then by historical accident or historical knowledge? The catastrophic events of 1857 that bring about her death stand in for Taylor's growing recognition that he has no social script for Seeta.

Her function in the plot reaches its culmination during an armed attack on the Mostyn residence when she throws herself before a spear aimed at Cyril by Azrael Pande who, full of hatred and vengeance, wants only to kill Cyril. She dies having achieved the apotheosis of the faithful and devoted Hindu wife who would give her life for her husband. Cyril, after a period of mourning, marries Grace Mostyn, and in the final scene of the novel, they gaze together at a picture of Seeta which hangs in their house. Seeta is transformed into an icon, a sentimental memento, elevated to a moral emblem after she transcends the historical deadlock of the narrative. Her death also gives Taylor the opportunity to demonstrate definitively the Indian woman's centrality to the construction of the figure of the good colonizer.

In an inversion of the chivalric ideal by which Cyril rescues Seeta from the bandits, the last third of the novel focuses on her sacrifice for him. As she lies dying, Taylor recalls again the absurdly abject image by which she is described at the beginning of the novel, "[Seeta] could only look at them, silently by turns, as a dog would at one it loved, and the great brown eyes seemed, for the time, full of warm soft light" (381). The dog-like eyes that suggest silent, unquestioning devotion are also a reminder of Seeta's consistent function in the novel—to define Cyril's nobility. She further abases herself in her dying words to him: "only forgive your wife that she was careless, negligent often, and so ignorant" (383). Seeta's death highlights the sadism inherent in the establishment of colonial authority that appears in the coercive mechanisms Taylor uses to bring the Rani of Shorapur to submission. The Rani's dying words to Taylor, as recorded in his memoir, recall Seeta's : "Will you forgive me all that I have done to you? I am a mean old woman. You are going one way, and I another; we shall never meet again" (266). By acknowledging their imperfections and submitting to the patriarchal figure of the Englishman, both women as native subjects affirm the justice and benevolence of colonial authority. In the moment of death, the narrative closure is effected by the final conversion of the women into obedient subjects, which also serves as a cathartic absolution of any guilt or blame for Cyril and Taylor.

The historical unconscious of the text points, then, to that other subject, the Rani of Shorapur, whose domestication is never perfectly accomplished, but who provides the occasion for Taylor to demonstrate and perform colonial power in relation to her. The family romance in the Rani's case produces a disobedient daughter/wife who manipulates her familial privilege to lay claim to state power and oppose patriarchal authority. The historical Rani struggles against being cast as the ideal ally of the British even though she performs abject dependency out of political expediency. Although Taylor's account dwells on his triumph over the Rani, her life and career leave him deeply dissatisfied with her as subject, as ally, and as a woman inhabiting her proper sphere. His fictional construct gives him the opportunity to refigure the obduracy of the Rani as the acquiescence of the native woman in the idealized world of *Seeta*. But the failure of this romance reveals not only the romantic figurations of the educable native that are deeply embedded in the ideology of colonialism, but also in the failed projects of liberal colonialism, the contradictions within its ideology.

CONCLUSION

Why Romance Matters

The ideology of romance presents love as the exceptional case which defies official rules governing social and sexual intermixing in any culture. The subversive potential of the exceptional case opens up many possibilities for arguing for the transformative potential of love plots, their questioning of received social norms, and their Utopian projection of possibilities in a world that denies them. I will return to the possibilities of romance later, but first I want to emphasize the importance of reading the romance as a record of social and political history. I return to William Dalrymple's *White Mughals,* a recent study of a romance set in eighteenth-century India, in which he presents interracial marriage as embedded in the political, social, and cultural relations of ruling British officials with the native aristocracy in the South Indian state of Hyderabad, though it is ultimately set apart from its context and in defiance of the governing social assumptions of that period. Surrounded by political intrigue, imperial ambition, and jostling for social power are the two lovers, the aristocratic Khair-un-nissa and James Kirkpatrick, British Resident at Hyderabad. Dalrymple's objective in his account of this late-eighteenth-century romance between an Englishman and his Indian wife, is to celebrate the synthesis of cultures, and the possibility of romance that crosses racial and cultural boundaries. He paints a picture of the tragic, sad, and ultimately wronged Khair-un-nissa betrayed by the perfidy of one Englishman, as much as she was loved and honored by Kirkpatrick. Against the backdrop of the aggressive policy of annexations instituted by Lord Wellesley, the racist premises that drove Company policy, and the uncultured approach of British officials to Indians in general, he shows the greatness of Kirkpatrick and the nobility of his love for Khair-un-nissa. In Dalrymple's account, the colonial context is more complex than segregated British and Indian cultures would suggest. In his introductory remarks, he points out that "the Kirkpatricks inhabited a world that was far more hybrid, and with far less clearly defined ethnic, national, and religious borders, than we have been conditioned to expect, either by conventional Imperial history books written in Britain before 1947, or by the nationalist historiography of post-Independence India, or for that matter by the postcolonial work coming from new generations of scholars, many of whom tend to follow the path opened up by Edward Said in his pioneering *Orientalism*" (Dalrymple xli). The romance, however, works ultimately to expose the colonial context in which it took place as close-minded, prejudiced, and driven by bigoted racial and cultural assumptions.

Dalrymple's declared objective in the subtitle of his *White Mughals* is to flesh out a tale of "love and betrayal in eighteenth-century India." His remarkable archival work in many languages provides a rich context in which to understand the story of Khair-un-nissa. But it is a tragic tale, and the early picture of Khair-un-nissa as someone who actively sought out Kirkpatrick and declared her love for him, gives way to a picture of a lonely young woman, who after the untimely death of Kirkpatrick is victimized by both her enemies at the court of the Nizam of Hyderabad and intolerant British officials. She is unable to return to Hyderabad to be with her mother nor does she have any desire to become a part of Anglo-Indian society in Calcutta, which, in any case, would have been hostile towards the Indian spouse of a British colonial official. At this difficult juncture in her life, she becomes entirely dependent on the friendship and patronage of Henry Russell, first assistant to James Kirkpatrick at the Residency at Hyderabad, and later Resident himself. This part of the story revolves around Russell's kindness to Khair and his eventual betrayal of her. In her final days, we see Khair as a betrayed lover, who pines away at the age of twenty-seven.

By keeping the focus on the idea of romance Dalrymple is able to highlight the nobility of Kirkpatrick even as he foregrounds political intrigue, social ferment, and economic enterprise in the background of this great romance. However, what stands out at the end is surely not the wonder of such an interracial romance taking place at all, but rather the impossibility of it. Structurally, politically, and socially, everything is ranged against Kirkpatrick and Khair-un-nissa once the marriage is accomplished. After Kirkpatrick's untimely death, Khair-un-nissa is unable to access the support of her family because of the enmity of a faction of the court of Hyderabad. When Henry Russell offers her his protection and in fact enters into a relationship with her, it causes a second round of consternation among British officials. Thomas Sydenham, Kirkpatrick's successor as Resident at Hyderabad, was courteous to Russell and Khair, but reluctant to grant Khair protection were she to return to Hyderabad with Russell. Sir George Barlow, senior member of Wellesley's Council, "was horrified by the new development" particularly because of its possible political consequences. He claimed a recent rebellion by Sepoys at Vellore had been caused by their anger at "the connexion of native women with European officers" (Dalrymple 433). Given that Kirkpatrick and Khair-un-nissa's relationship had already left a trail of acrimonious discussions, accusations, and defenses, the situation could hardly be expected to improve after his death. The narrative highlights the intense cruelty of both British colonial and Hyderabadi officials towards a woman who, in Dalrymple's narrative, has fortune, beauty, and courage: all the attributes of a heroine of romance.

Writing about her life in Calcutta after Kirkpatrick's death, Dalrymple comments, "There is absolutely no question of Khair-un-nissa being some sort of powerless ex-concubine: this is a beautiful, charismatic Mughal noblewoman behaving according to her rank, with a pair of senior British officials running around to do her bidding" (Dalrymple 425). Far from being a helpless damsel in distress, Khair-un-nissa took charge of the social and organizational aspects of her family in Hyderabad, which at this point consisted of her mother and her grandmother. Henry Russell was very responsive to her and accommodated most of her requests about communicating with her family and the court in Hyderabad. It is certainly true that Khair had the confidence and presence of someone who belonged to an upper-class family, and probably never thought of herself as a mere concubine but as someone who brought social power and privilege to the marriage. But her marriage to Kirkpatrick involves for her a loss of power and social standing. She is ultimately bereft of the networks of social influence that she would have had as an aristocratic Muslim woman. Further, her story highlights the continuing prejudice against mixed marriages in colonial India, both in the British community and in the courtly society of Hyderabad. The romance between her and Kirkpatrick thus becomes an exception rather than representative of relations between the communities. The exceptional nature of this romance suggests, however, the Utopian possibilities of crossing over, of bridging cultural divides, of feeling and commitment that grow despite official and social ideologies.

For another instance of the provocative, inflammatory, and ultimately Utopian potential of the romance, I turn now to an episode from contemporary India. In a thematically appropriate segue, this episode pertains to a contemporary cinematic rendering of the life of another Mughal, the sixteenth-century emperor Akbar, in a movie entitled *Jodha Akbar*, which was released in India in February 2008. Akbar is widely regarded in popular mythology and historical accounts as the most tolerant and liberal among Mughals. The expansion of his empire over large parts of India was accompanied by an inclusive and liberal view of religion. To add to this egalitarian mix was the fact that he married a Hindu princess from among the clans of Rajputs, rulers of small states and principalities in Central India, and among the strongest opponents of the Mughals. This marriage of alliance, which, in folklore was a happy one, elevated his Rajput wife to a position of great influence, especially after she became the mother of the heir to his throne. Historians quarrel with popular accounts and cinematic representations over her name—Jodha Bai—which they argue was incorrectly given to this particular princess when in fact there is more evidence to suggest that it belonged to her son Jahangir's wife. Regardless of the controversy over the actual name and identity of this Hindu princess, the movie, filmed as a lavish period piece with celebrity actors in the lead, has enjoyed tremendous success at the box office. The supposed distortion of history, however, has aroused the ire of right-wing Hindu groups in large parts of North and Central India. They have called for a ban on the movie; subsequently a ban was imposed in a few states. The matter went up to the Supreme Court which lifted the ban on screening the film in some places, though it remains in place in many Indian states.

From some of the comments made by the protesting groups, it is easy to conclude that the real issue is not the correct name of the princess involved in the story, but the idea of love between a medieval Muslim prince and a Hindu princess recreated on the screen in sensuous detail. This has offended the sensibilities of a population engorged on a diet of violent Hindu-Muslim conflict during the past two decades. Their anger at the misrepresentation of history was further aggravated by the filmmaker Ashutosh Gowariker's insistence that the film was based on his historical research on the cities of Delhi, Jaipur, and Agra, important sites of the Mughal empire. Gowariker explicitly mentions the absence of any stories about Jodha Bai in all the historical writing about Akbar, which then inspired him to make her the focus of his film about the life of the Mughal emperor.[1]

Responding to the furor over the historical accuracy of the events in the film, historians have pointed out that she is not present in any of the Persian chronicles about Akbar's reign. They do, however, agree that the historical record confirms that Akbar married a Rajput princess of the kingdom of Amer, though her name was not Jodha.[2] From the historian's point of view, this projection of an egalitarian, proto-feminist Jodha is as anachronistic as the emphasis on Hindu-Muslim harmony. In sixteenth-century India, Rajputs often contracted marriages with Muslims, and many of these were, as in other parts of the medieval world, ways of making political alliances, negotiating peace, or acknowledging the sovereignty of the ascendant power. Hindu-Muslim differences would not have stood out as much as they are made to in the film rendering of this particular interreligious marriage. Caste, clan, and lineage were much more important in the medieval world than distinct religious identities. It is important to remind ourselves that many of the identities that we privilege in the modern world were created by colonial regimes. The reification of caste and religious identities was in large part caused by colonial taxonomies which were then funneled into modern political constituencies. In that sense, it is a point well taken that it is *our* great need to highlight differences and resolve them in romance narratives in order to restore sanity to our conflicted world, but that these differences were not the primary categories in which identities were recognized in the world of Jodha and Akbar.[3]

In a strange convergence between left-wing academic historians and Hindu groups, the concern with the accuracy of the historical record has dominated much of the controversy around the movie. It is even more ironic that Hindu groups concerned with the accuracy of historical facts have been mired in controversy in India and the United States over the revision of school history textbooks that, according to them, portray Hindu culture and religion in a negative light. Sometimes going against the work of academic historians, the community has sought to take charge of the version of Hindu history which will be handed down to their children, thereby making it transparent that all versions of history have a political and ideological position.

Jodha Akbar appears in my concluding remarks because it is once again a strong reminder of the power of a romance plot to suggest possibilities of social and political alliance and unanticipated networks of desire, which make up the immense unknown possibilities of human connection and commitment. While those concerned with an accurate rendering of the history of glorious Rajput kingdoms protest that Akbar's wife had a different name, others see the film as reflecting political and social concerns of contemporary India. They have been content to forgo the quibble over Jodha's real name to celebrate the secular and nonsectarian vision of the film and its portrayal of the romance between religious groups that have been murderously hostile to each other in contemporary India. In language that evokes Doris Sommer's conception of the romance as an allegory of political reconciliation, the sociologist, Shiv Viswanathan celebrates the film's "romance of unity and integration.... There is a passion and power in this unity (in diversity), which is what contemporary India needs."[4] The Danish anthropologist Stine Simonsen Puri reads another kind of cultural lesson in the recreation of this medieval Hindu-Muslim romance. For her, it is an example of how a negotiation of identity can happen while opening oneself to another culture.[5] Jodha insists on having her own Hindu temple and on following Hindu festivals and ceremonies while living in the house of her Muslim husband at the same time that she participates in the cultural life of his extended household.

This romance appeals to the popular imagination just as nineteenth-century interracial romances did to their vast audiences. The director of *Jodha Akbar* admitted, despite his earlier claims to historical accuracy, that he ultimately based his depiction of Jodha on "popular usage."[6] The legend of Jodha Bai has become attached to Akbar in the popular imagination, and Hindi films depicting that era of Indian history have perpetuated the idea of a romantic, companionate marriage between the two. It could well be that the reason none of the Persian chronicles of Akbar's times mention Jodha is that they were operating within their own conventions of recording what was considered significant history, and women did not figure in it.[7] It is the achievement of modern historiography and theory that we can interrogate archival and recorded history and bring such absences to light.

The controversy over bringing to cinematic life a neglected figure from history in an interreligious romance demonstrates not only the discontents of contemporary sectarian politics but also the Utopian possibilities of romance. As Sharmishta Gooptu points out in her review of *Jodha Akbar*, historical anachronisms apart, the significance of this contemporary rendering of a romance lies in "its power to make the past relevant to the present through the mechanics of pleasure and the imagination" (Gooptu 2). The creation of romance fantasies thus does important cultural and political work. Readers of Anglo-Indian romances thrived on vicarious transgressions of racial boundaries and the pleasures of imagining an unconventional domestic life. These romances set up complex patterns of identification and rejection in their representation of cultural difference and racial otherness. The function of the romance is thus not just critical, but also creative. Romances that traffic in history are compelling and subversive because they present alternative possibilities of social, political, and cultural connection that both excite and disturb us. This is why a complex engagement with different forms of romance not only enriches our understanding of the nineteenth-century colonial world, but is as urgent and necessary an enterprise for our contemporary globalizing, multicultural world, preoccupied as it is with matters of "difference."

NOTES

INTRODUCTION

1. A word commonly used to refer to an Indian wife, mistress, or companion of a European man in colonial India.

2. See Llewellyn-Jones, Rosie, *A Very Ingenious Man: Claude Martin in Early Colonial India*.

3. The term "family romance" usually recalls Freud's concept that refers to a childhood dream of class mobility in which the child replaces through fantasies of adoption his or her parents with others who are wealthier and more powerful than they. See Jean Laplanche and J. B. Pontalis, *The Language of Psycho-analysis* 160.

4. "Anglo-Indian" is a term used to describe the British community in colonial India. It was only in the census of 1911 that the Government of British India made it the official term for "Eurasian" or person of mixed white and native Asian descent.

5. Kipling is reported to have been working on such a full-length study entitled "Mother Maturin." His other short stories on the subject of interracial love are "Beyond the Pale," "Yoked to an Unbeliever," and "Lispeth." See McBratney, *Imperial Subjects, Imperial Space: Rudyard Kipling's Fiction of the Native-Born* 51 and 182.

6. In other colonial contexts, racially "other" women have been studied through the thematics of sexual pathology (the Hottentot Venus), the misogynist tropes of a threatening and voracious femininity (the Yahoo woman), or as victims of social barbarism (in harems in Near and Middle Eastern cultures, for instance). Sander Gilman, in his "Black Bodies, White Bodies: Toward an Iconography of Female Sexuality in Late Nineteenth-Century Art, Medicine, and Literature," discusses the fascination with the Hottentot Venus in nineteenth-century England. The Yahoo woman appears in Book IV of Jonathan Swift's *Gulliver's Travels*. For a discussion

of representations of native women in this and other eighteenth-century texts, see Laura Brown, *Ends of Empire: Women and Ideology in Early Eighteenth-Century English Literature*; Felicity Nussbaum *Torrid Zones: Maternity, Sexuality, and Empire in Eighteenth-Century English Narratives*; and Shirley Samuels, *Romances of the Republic*.

7. Davidoff and Hall describe, for instance, the "flexible make-up and permeable boundaries" of the family. See their *Family Fortunes* 36.

8. Mary Poovey writes that "the middle-class ideology we most often associate with the Victorian period was both contested and always under construction; because it was always in the making, it was always open to revision, dispute, and the emergence of oppositional formulations" (*Uneven Developments* 3). Elizabeth Langland in *Nobody's Angels* makes the case that "with the rapid increase of wealth generated by the industrial revolution and the consequent social upheavals, status became a fluid thing, increasingly dependent upon the manipulation of social signs" (26).

9. See Indrani Chatterjee, *Gender, Slavery, and Law in Colonial India*, especially 78–124.

10. See Chatterjee 102. Another example of the active role that a woman tried to play in the administration of her estate is the case of the Rani of Burdwan, who, though ultimately defeated by the Company, resisted, protested, intrigued, and won a few rounds of the battle between her faction and advisors appointed by the Company. For a detailed account of this struggle, see John R. McLane, *Land and Local Kingship in Eighteenth-Century Bengal* 223–66.

11. In "Making Empire Respectable: The Politics of Race and Sexual Morality in 20th-Century Colonial Cultures," Stoler writes that by the early twentieth century "local women who had been considered protectors of men's well-being, were now seen as the bearers of ill health and sinister influences; adaptation to local food, language, and dress, once prescribed as healthy signs of acclimatization, were now sources of contagion and loss of (white) self" (56). In her other essays, Stoler shows how concubinage in many European colonies acquired a different political charge in different periods of colonial history. Initially local women were seen as important sources of knowledge, inexpensive managers of the colonial household, and a means of sexual release. See also Stoler's "Carnal Knowledge and Imperial Power: Gender, Race, and Morality in Colonial Asia."

12. Commenting on the social life in British India between 1786 and 1793, Mildred Archer writes that in that period many of the older Company servants lived settled lives with unofficial Indian wives or bibis. See her *India and British Portraiture* 50–51. The only other instance of official "management" of such relationships in India was in the case of brothels for soldiers posted in Northern India. See Kenneth Ballhatchet's *Race, Sex and Class under the Raj*, in which he claims that the British made a distinction between the proclivities of the lower and upper classes and hence "provided" for the soldiers whose sexual desires required official management through the setting up of brothels and lock hospitals, i.e. hospitals set up for the treatment of syphilis. See Ballhatchet 10–39.

13. A notable exception is Nancy Paxton's *Writing under the Raj*. Sangeeta Ray notes in *Engendering India* that the Indian woman disrupts the Victorian family romance, but does not pursue this idea any further. In *Allegories of Empire: The Figure of Woman in the Colonial Text*, Jenny Sharpe notes the absence of the Indian woman in allegories of sexual and racial violence. Although Sharpe "makes a case

for the figure of woman being instrumental in shifting a colonial system of meaning from self-interest and moral superiority to self-sacrifice and racial superiority" (7), thereby touching on the concept of "benevolent colonialism," her project is a study of the "the place of the colonial text in a feminist recovery of *European women's history*" (8; my emphasis). Kate Teltscher devotes an entire chapter to representations of Indian women in her *India Inscribed: European and British Writing on India 1600–1800*, but her focus is on Orientalist conceptions of highly sexual harem women or Hindu women engaged in horrific heathen practices.

14. John McBratney points out, for instance, that in Kipling's few interracial romances, the Indian woman is figured as an engulfing, destructive presence that has to be rejected so that the integrity of the British empire can be preserved (*Imperial Subjects* 71).

15. See Gayatri Spivak, "Three Women's Texts and a Critique of Imperialism" (1986) and Edward Said's discussion of *Mansfield Park*, "Jane Austen and Empire," in his *Culture and Imperialism* 80–97.

16. See Jenny Sharpe, *Allegories of Empire*; Suvendrini Perera, *Reaches of Empire*; Susan Meyer, *Imperialism at Home*; and Deirdre David, *Rule Britannia*.

17. The challenge of such work is to be interdisciplinary at a particular site of empire. The methodological and theoretical challenges of interdisciplinary colonial studies have been admirably met in a recent anthology such as *A New Imperial History*, the originality of which lies in the fact that it draws from scholars who work in many different disciplines, asking questions and covering areas of colonial studies that fall between lines of disciplinary inquiry or that had never found a place in canonized fields of research. Kathleen Wilson, in her introduction to the volume, points out that "empire affected the most quotidian as well as the most momentous aspects of everyday life, cultural production, sociability and identity . . . " (21). Moving beyond the concerns of history alone, these scholars also take up "the role of representation in enabling, mystifying, and contesting British imperial power" (18–19). By studying different kinds of representation—whether it is the colonial epistle or colonial self-presentation through attire—the essays in this volume construct a microhistory of empire that relies for its narratives on "competing fragments" of history and cross-disciplinary debates.

18. For an extended discussion of this idea, see Karen Chase and Michael Levenson, *The Spectacle of Intimacy* 181–200.

19. By the term "Orientalist," I mean the group of philologists, historians, and linguists, primarily at the Asiatic Society, founded in Calcutta in 1784 by Warren Hastings. The other prominent members of this group were William Jones, who "discovered" the golden age of Hindu civilization; H. T. Colebrook; William Carey; H. H. Wilson; and John Prinsep. See David Kopf, *British Orientalism and the Bengal Renaissance*. The main assumptions of this Orientalist history were that in ancient Hindu, Vedic civilization, literature and the arts flourished, society was affluent and peaceful, women occupied a place of honor in social and familial structures, and the hegemony of Brahmanic culture prevailed. The subsequent decline in the social status of women was indicative of a general social decline.

20. See Uma Chakravarti, "Whatever Happened to the Vedic *Dasi*?: Orientalism, Nationalism, and a Script for the Past," in *Recasting Women* 27–87. Chakravarti argues that "it is no wonder that the Vedic dasi (woman in servitude), captured, subjugated, and enslaved by the conquering Aryans, but who also represents one

aspect of Indian womanhood, disappeared without leaving a trace of herself in nineteenth century history" (28). This disappearance of the female slave allowed the Orientalists to make sweeping claims about the high status of all women in that period.

21. For a study of the legal and cultural history of Sati in colonial India, see Lata Mani, "Contentious Traditions" 126, and "Production of an Official Discourse on Sati in Early Nineteenth-Century Bengal." Mani's work constitutes the single largest contribution to an understanding of Sati as embedded in colonial discourses of government, legal history, and social reform. In her analysis of parliamentary papers and official documents, Mani points out that one of the main assumptions that informed the debates on Sati was "the hegemonic status accorded by colonial officials to brahmanic scriptures in the organization of social life" ("Production" 91).

22. Uma Chakravarti points to a classic and influential example of this preoccupation with the upper-caste Hindu widow. In Henry Colebrook's first research article, "On the Duties of the Faithful Hindu Widow," published posthumously in *Asiatic Researches* in 1894, "predictably, the focal starting point was the ritual of Sati" (Chakravarti 31). Speculating on the impact of this article on the European readers of the journal, she says:

> For many decades thereafter a reference to Hindus appears to have evoked the image of a burning woman as recorded by Max Muller almost eighty years later. Whatever other research Colebrook engaged himself with in reconstructing the 'glories' of the ancient Hindus, an unintended consequence of his essay on the 'faithful' Hindu widow was to add the weight of scholarship to the accounts of travelers and other lay writers whose descriptions of burning women came to represent an integral part of the perception of Indian reality. Colebrook's account of Sati highlighted an 'awesome' aspect of Indian womanhood, carrying both the associations of a barbaric society and of the mystique of the Hindu woman who 'voluntarily' and 'cheerfully' mounted the funeral pyre of her husband. (Chakravarti 31)

23. Warren Hastings (1732–1818) was Governor of Bengal from 1772 and the first Governor-General of the British territories in India from 1774 to 1785. He was impeached for corruption in 1787, but acquitted in 1795. For a discussion of the trial of Warren Hastings, see Frans de Bruyn, "Edmund Burke's Gothic Romance: The Portrayal of Warren Hastings in Burke's Writings and Speeches on India"; Sara Suleri, *The Rhetoric of English India* 49–74; and Siraj Ahmed, "The Theater of the Civilized Self: Edmund Burke and the East India Trials."

24. In "The Theater of the Civilized Self," Siraj Ahmed argues that passages about the cruelty to women in Burke's speeches to British Parliament show that in Burke's view "the establishment of colonial rule in British India reverses the narrative of civil society" (37).

25. Sara Suleri warns readers against positing a simple gendered alterity in the colonized landscape (*Rhetoric* 16). Her dissatisfaction with the gendering of colonized land stems from her conception of the colonial relation in the metaphor of rape. I argue for the rich metaphoric potential of the Indian woman in heterosexual romances.

26. In her study the French Revolution, Lynn Hunt argues that "the French had a kind of collective political unconscious that was structured by narratives of family relations.... The revolutionary family romances were not neurotic reactions to disappointment—as in Freud's formulation—but creative efforts to reimagine the political world, to reimagine a polity unhinged from patriarchal authority" (Hunt xiii).

27. Jyotsna Singh in *Colonial Narratives, Cultural Dialogues* identifies "the tropes of discovery, civilization, and rescue" as defining the language of colonization, and, in fact, surviving beyond that era (5). She also describes this motif as one of the primary "strategies and themes" of British colonialism together with "discovering, civilizing . . . and cataloguing the Indian empire" (4).

28. Gayatri Spivak, "Can the Subaltern Speak?" 297. Spivak is referring to the British abolition of the practice of Sati, which for them became an index of the state of Indian society at that time.

29. Intellectual historians have also been hard put to establish the exact value of the tropes in which White has suggested that history is conceptualized. These are the tropes of Romance, Tragedy, Comedy, and Satire. The priority of these tropes in organizing historical thinking has been the subject of much debate. As Wulf Kansteiner asks, "should the tropes be considered as preconceptual figures of thought which already determine the initial processing of the material, or are they more adequately described as master concepts which only guide the writing process proper, the actual emplotting of the facts?" (281). See Wulf Kansteiner, "Hayden White's Critique of the Writing of History."

30. See Kalle Pihlainen's compelling exposition on the literature-history debate that arose from Hayden White's writings in "The Moral of the Historical Story," especially 51–57. I am indebted to this essay for its description of the trajectory of White's ideas.

PART I

1. Another side of interracial sexual commerce, which was also considered equally disruptive, is represented by organized prostitution in the regimental brothels. As Kenneth Ballhatchet has shown, these were attached to army barracks and were regulated to provide the soldiers easy access to women, who were kept under the surveillance of the state so that disease could be prevented or contained. See Kenneth Ballhatchet, *Race, Sex, and Class under the Raj* 14.

2. Mildred Archer's *India and British Portraiture* presents a detailed picture of the social history of the Presidencies in the late eighteenth century. See especially 51.

3. S. C. Ghosh reproduces the wills of many British men that provide for their Indian wives and natural children. See Appendix III in *The Social Condition of the British Community in Bengal 1757–1800*.

4. See Durba Ghosh 109.

5. Thomas Williamson in *East India Vademecum*. Quoted in Archer, *India and British Portraiture* 51.

6. Quoted in Dennis Holman, *Sikander Sahib: The Life of Colonel James Skinner, 1778–1841* 7.

7. P. J. Marshall points out that "in most morphologies of colonies, India is portrayed as the classic 'colony of exploitation' by contrast with 'colonies of settlement,' such as Australia" (29).

8. Percival Spear, *The Nabobs: A Study of the Social Life of the English in Eighteenth-Century India* 12.

9. Spear gives the exact numbers: "In 1678–79, there were 74 Company's servants in Madras; only six were married and had their wives with them. One of the wives was English, one Dutch, two English half-castes, and two Portuguese. In addition, there were six widows and two unmarried ladies in the settlement and sixteen other Europeans in white or black town" (*Nabobs* 13).

10. S. C. Ghosh points out that the total number of marriages even after 1757 was very low. He takes his evidence from Bengal where between 1757 and 1800, 1 in 4 writers (junior clerks in the Company), 1 in 10 cadets, 1 in 15 to 1 in 45 of the other ranks, and 1 in 8 of nonofficial Europeans married (*Social Condition* 59).

11. S. C. Ghosh presents the following figures: in 1756, there were 671 European men to 80 women, in 1810, 4000 European men to 250 European women in Bengal (*Social Condition* 53).

12. David Kopf in *British Orientalism and the Bengal Renaissance* describes late-eighteenth-century Orientalists as existing in a "cross-cultural vacuum" (15). Even though relations between the two communities were marked by a certain freedom and informality, the British in India at that time "were alien freebooters longing to return home shouldering their bags of riches" (15).

13. See Ronald Hyam, *Empire and Sexuality* 117. For disparaging attitudes towards Eurasians, see Ballhatchet 96–122.

14. See Clement Hawes, *Poor Relations: The Making of a Eurasian Community in British India 1773–1833* 133–49.

15. Durba Ghosh comes to this conclusion from the wills of British men in which they make provisions for their dependents. See Ghosh 118.

16. The word comes from "nawab," a Muslim aristocrat usually attached to the court or a member of a ruling family. This was adopted into English as "nabob" in the eighteenth century.

17. Perceval Spear dismisses hybridity by saying that smoking hookahs (hubble-bubble pipes) and chewing pan (betel leaf) did not suggest that the *English* community was coming closer to the mainstream of Indian life (*The Nabobs* 2).

18. See Nikos Papastergiadis, "Tracing Hybridity in Theory" 259, for this argument.

19. Hyam, "*Empire*" 116–17.

CHAPTER ONE

1. All letters will henceforth be cited by their dates.

2. Although the original manuscript of the Gardner Papers in the Oriental and India Office Collections in the British Museum are illegible, there is a typed transcript of these letters in the National Army Museum in London. My chapter is based on a reconstruction of the original manuscript with assistance from this typed manuscript.

3. See *Dictionary of National Biography*. Ed Leslie Stephen and Sir Sidney Lee, vol. vii. Oxford: Oxford University Press, 1921–22, 873.

4. See William Dalrymple, *White Mughals* 201–203, 275–76, and 358–61.

5. Lionel Gardner's *The Sabre and the Spur* is the only complete biography of William Linneaus Gardner. The Gardner family to this day sends one son from each generation to lead the army corps set up by William Linneaus. Lionel Gardner lives in Chandigarh in North India.

6. *Gardner Papers*, Letter to his aunt Mrs Lostock, May 25, 1815, Cambridge South Asia Archive.

7. See Dalrymple 180–90.

8. Oriental and India Office Collections, British Library, London, Kirkpatrick Papers, Mss Eur F228/83, Hyderabad, 23 May 1800.

9. See Index to Bengal Will, British Library, London L/AG/34/29/57 Parts 3 & 4 (1 Oct.–31 Dec. 1835).

10. See the correspondence between James Kirkpatrick, his brother William Kirkpatrick, and Lord Wellesely in 1802 in the British Library IOL Eur. Mss. F 228/83 collection.

11. See Roslyn Jolly, "Stevenson's 'Sterling Domestic Fiction,' *The Beach of Falesá*," in which she argues that Stevenson's representation of interracial marriage between the English Wiltshire and the Polynesian Uma calls into questions the separation between adventure and domesticity, romance and realism, and between races.

12. Robert Young's *Colonial Desire* has excellent discussions of the influence of three works on ideas about racial mixing and its consequences for culture: Robert Knox's *The Races of Men* (1850), Count Gobineau's *Essay on the Inequality of Races* (1853–55), and Edward Long's *History of Jamaica* (1774). See *Colonial Desire* 14–17, 99–109, and 150–51, respectively.

13. Compare this with Dalrymple's speculation about Khair-un-nissa's views on similar issues: "Khair-un-nissa, one can presume, would have insisted on all the basic traditional ceremonies being performed for her children . . . nor does James seem likely to have opposed his children being brought up as Muslims (340).

14. Also spelled as Begum Samru, and known as Zeb-un-nissa and Joanna Nobilis Somers. She lived from 1750–1836 and was the ruler of the small principality of Sardhana in North India. Aditya Behl writes that "she drew freely on European and Indian models of behaviour and legitimation of authority," and was part of "a distinctively mixed culture that she helped create in northern India." See Aditya Behl, "Articulating a Life, in Words and Pictures: Begum Samru and *The Ornament of Histories*" 100. See also Michael Fisher, "Becoming and Making 'Family' in Hindustan."

15. Dalrymple, 496.

16. See Ram Babu Saksena, *The Indo-British Poets of Urdu and Persian* 113 for a copy of James Valentine Gardner's will.

CHAPTER TWO

1. For studies of the imperial theme in Victorian domestic fiction, see Gayatri Spivak, Patrick Brantlinger, Susan Meyer, Dierdre David, Rajeswari Sunder Rajan,

and Jenny Sharpe. But while studies of canonical authors such as Jane Austen, Charlotte Brontë, Charles Dickens, and W. M. Thackeray have taken this injunction very seriously, literature generated in the colonies has not been studied with the same urgency.

2. My argument is influenced by Roslyn Jolly's study of Robert Louis Stevenson's *The Beach of Falesa*, which, she argues, is a hybrid genre in which Stevenson rejects the values and generic properties of the colonial adventure to adopt the "feminine realm of domestic fiction." She shows that his representation of interracial marriage between the English Wiltshire and the Polynesian Uma calls into question the separation between adventure and domesticity, romance and realism, and between races. See R. Jolly, "Stevenson's 'Sterling Domestic Fiction,' *The Beach of Falesá*" 463. Other texts that have been discussed in these terms include H. Rider Haggard's *She* and *King Solomon's Mines*, and Joseph Conrad's *Lord Jim* and *Heart of Darkness*. See Anne McClintock, *Imperial Leather* 240–48.

3. Most studies of Anglo-Indian domesticity focus on the "women's sphere" as constituted by *memsahibs* or wives of British civil servants. See Rosemary George, *The Politics of Home;* Alison Sainsbury, "Married to the Empire: The Anglo-Indian Domestic Novel"; and Margaret Stieg, "Indian Romances: Tracts for the Times." A recent exception is Nancy Paxton's *Writing under the Raj*. A second set of writings on Anglo-Indian culture also focus on the role of white women in India. These include Barbara Ramusack's "Cultural Missionaries, Maternal Imperialists, Feminist Allies" and Antoinette M. Burton's "The White Woman's Burden: British Feminists and 'The Indian Woman,' 1865–1915."

4. Paxton explores stock Indian figures such as evil queens, dancing girls, and intriguing residents of the *zenana* or harems who can be seen as the antithesis of the self-immolating and faithful Sati. However, in her reading of interracial marriages Paxton focuses more on literary narratives about relationships between "New Women" and Indian men than on the dynamics of relationships between Englishmen and Indian women.

5. All references to these two novels are from Bithia Mary Croker, *The Company's Servant: A Romance of Southern India*. Leipzig, Bernhard Tauchnitz, 1908 and *In Old Madras*. Leipzig, Bernhard Tauchnitz, 1913. Page numbers follow cited text.

6. As Abena Busia has argued, *Heart of Darkness* is posited on the silencing of the African woman, and hence the erasure of miscegenation. See her "Miscegenation as Metonymy: Sexuality and Power in the Colonial Novel."

7. For a descriptive account of this genre see Margaret Stieg and Alison Sainsbury.

8. Bhupal Singh, *A Survey of Anglo-Indian Fiction*.

9. Quoted in Wolff, ed., *Nineteenth-Century Fiction*, vol. I: 319.

10. The founder, Baron Tauchnitz, described as a "fervent Anglophile," is said to have declared that "As a German-Saxon it gave me particular pleasure to promote the literary interest of my Anglo-Saxon cousins, by rendering English literature as universally known as possible beyond the limits of the British Empire" (Todd and Bowden vii).

11. On its frontispiece, Croker's *In Old Madras* declares: "The Copyright of this Collection is purchased for Continental Circulation only, and the volumes may therefore not be introduced into Great Britain or her Colonies."

12. See Stoler, "Making Empire Respectable." Anna Davin and Hanneke Ming also argue that interracial marriage and its management were central to colonial cultures in Africa and Southeast Asia, respectively. See A. Davin, "Imperialism and Motherhood" and H. Ming, "Barracks Concubinage in the Indies, 1887–1920."

13. Alison Sainsbury traces the English heritage of the Anglo-Indian romance to "the 'domestic novel,' focused on women's activities in the home, the sentimental novel, with its defence of virginity, and the gothic novel, whose 'exotic' settings betoken threat" (163).

14. Gary R. Dyer borrows the term "low-Other" from Peter Stallybrass and Allon White's *The Politics and Poetics of Transgression*. He analyzes the bourgeois criticism of charity bazaars in London as arising from a perception of the bazaar as a place of commercialism, Eastern influence, and feminine corruption. See his "The 'Vanity Fair' of Nineteenth-Century England: Commerce, Women, and the East in the Ladies' Bazaar."

15. See John Sutherland's introduction to *The New Nineteenth Century: Feminist Readings of Underread Victorian Fiction*. Also see Lyn Pykett's "Afterword" and articles by Toni Johnson-Woods and Gail Turley Houston in *Beyond Sensation: Mary Elizabeth Braddon in Context*. Another collection which emphasizes reader response and underscores the fact that such fiction could both endorse and subvert ideological norms it represents, is *Feminist Readings of Victorian Popular Texts*.

PART II

1. Though there was no unified notion of the colonial State in India at least in the first half of the nineteenth century, the policies of the East India Company on most issues were directed by uniform principles and in effect functioned as a form of state power.

2. For a detailed discussion of these debates see C. C. Elridge, *England's Mission*.

3. See Lata Mani, *Contentious Traditions;* Gauri Viswanathan, *Masks of Conquest;* and Mrinalini Sinha, *Colonial Masculinity*.

4. See Sudipta Sen, "Liberal Empire and Illiberal Trade: The Political Economy of 'Responsible Government' in Early British India."

5. Paramountcy changed and evolved as a policy through the nineteenth century. Though the groundwork for annexations was laid by Governors-General Cornwallis (1786–1793) and Richard Wellesley (1798–1805), I am concerned mainly with the tenure of Dalhousie (1848–1856). After Dalhousie's aggressive annexations, which were perceived by some to have caused the revolt of 1857, Queen Victoria announced in 1858 that the earlier treaties and agreements with the native princes would be honored by the British government which took over direct administration of India, thereby ending the rule of the East India Company. Annexations did not really stop after 1858, and as Ian Copland points out, 1890–1914 was a period of the reconstruction of Paramountcy. See his *The British Raj and the Indian Princes*.

6. Sri Nandan Prasad points out in *Paramountcy under Dalhousie* that as a political equation, Paramountcy was unique to India and unlike other such political

relationships, such as the Romanization of subordinate states in Imperial Rome or, closer home, the feudal relationship between the Mughals and their vassals.

7. See Michael Fisher's *Indirect Rule in India* 30. This is the most detailed study of the Residents as part of a coherent system of governance in India.

CHAPTER THREE

1. Other works of this kind would include two works by J. W. Kaye, *The Administration of the East India Company: A History of Indian Progress* (1853) and *A History of the Sepoy War in India 1857-58*. See also Edwin Arnold, *The Marquis of Dalhousie's Administration of British India*. Nineteenth-century observers such as Charles Jackson, member of the Governor-General's council in his *A Vindication of the Marquis of Dalhousie's Indian Administration* (1865), and William Lee-Warner in his *The Protected Princes of India* (1894), both defend Dalhousie's policy of annexation. Later historians question the legality and wisdom of these annexations and point to the injustice perpetrated on the widows of the deceased kings as a consequence of these annexations, although they do not make a simplistic connection between Dalhousie's doctrine of lapse and the Revolt of 1857. M. A. Rahim's *Lord Dalhousie's Administration of the Conquered and Annexed States* (1963) makes an admirable case for this point of view. B. D. Basu's *The Story of Satara* (1922) is cast as a eulogy of the dead king in which the condition of the hapless widow is used as an emotionally charged instance of the ruthlessness of the colonial regime. None analyzes the strategies by which the queens negotiated their right to power and personal property with the East India Company, a process that questioned Victorian ideologies of gender.

2. See Robert Travers, *Ideology and Empire in Eighteenth-Century India*, especially 128-29 for this point. Travers notes "these [land] disputes suggest both how the political revolutions of recent years had contributed to an unsettled environment for land rights, and also that female landholders may have been especially vulnerable to attacks to their rights" (128).

3. It is important to note here that this dispute happened at a time soon after the passing of the Regulating Act of 1773 by which British Parliament sought to reorganize and regulate the affairs of the Company and restrain its excesses. A new five-man Supreme Council was nominated and for the first time a Crown court, the Supreme Court, presided over by British judges, would sit in Calcutta and have jurisdiction over 'His Majesty's subjects in India.' The supervisory function of the Council inevitably created tensions with the Company government of Bengal, which saw the members of the Council as meddlesome outsiders. See Travers 143-80.

4. See a detailed discussion of this case in Travers 191-200.

5. This is a point famously made by Lata Mani in her discussion of the self-immolating widow or Sati. She argues that the debates around the abolition of Sati demonstrated most dramatically the centrality of the "native woman" to the definition and exercise of patriarchal authority, both British and Indian. The Sati, who evoked both horror and admiration in England, became a poignant image for the need for enlightened British rule which would save the Hindu widow from a

horrible fate. East India Company policy, on the other hand, dictated restraint and caution in dealing with such socio-religious controversies.

6. See Joseph 140–41.
7. See Prem Chowdhry, "Customs in a Peasant Economy" 316.
8. See note 9, Introduction.
9. Banka Bai was to be given Rs. 120,000; the eldest Rani Rs. 50,000; and each of the remaining Ranis Rs. 25,000. Appa Sahib's widow was to be given Rs. 10,000 and the other women Rs. 20,000 as annual life pensions (qtd. in Rahim 249).
10. Rahim does not mention how this petition was received or whether the Rani was given back some or all her personal property. This, to me, is also indicative of the fact that British negotiations with these women have been relegated to the margins of history and do not inform social and cultural histories of this period.
11. In his edited collection *The Politics of the British Annexation of India*, Michael Fisher includes three letters written by the Rani Lakshmibai of Jhansi to the Marquis of Dalhousie protesting against the annexation of Jhansi. All references to these letters are from this edition.
12. Joyce Lebra-Chapman offers a detailed account of the birth of the legend of the Rani which refers to British and Indian reports of the Rani's last battle. See *The Rani of Jhansi* 114–17.

CHAPTER FOUR

1. This was edited and completed by his daughter in 1874.
2. Henry Reeve was a prominent writer on foreign affairs for *The Times*, and encouraged Taylor to write on India for the same newspaper. Taylor's letters to him were written between 1840 and 1849. In these letters, Taylor allows himself the license of close friendship to comment freely on Indian politics, and the foibles of Indian administrators and politicians.
3. For other discussions of this novel, which discuss the complexities of Meadows Taylor's colonial relationship with him, see Patrick Brantlinger, *Rule of Darkness* 86–90; Javed Majeed, "Meadows Taylor's *Confessions of a Thug*: The Anglo-Indian Novel as a Genre in the Making; Parama Roy, "Discovering India, Imagining Thuggee"; and Mary Poovey, "Ambiguity and Historicism: Interpreting Confessions of a Thug."
4. I am not proposing here that Taylor's literary work simply reflects his public life, even though he invites us to make that assumption when he claims in his introduction to *Seeta* that this novel is based on an incident that took place in his district court.
5. Title given to the Muslim ruler of Hyderabad.
6. Taylor seems to have been an Orientalist of the old school who developed a taste for Indian literature and respect for indigenous knowledge. David Kopf, discussing the process of acculturation of the British, writes that late-eighteenth-century Orientalists existed in a "cross-cultural vacuum" (15). Even though relations between the two communities were marked by a certain freedom and informality, the British in India at that time "were alien freebooters longing to return home shouldering their bags of riches" (15). In his view, the establishment of the College

of Fort William in 1800 inaugurated a period of acculturation, when a network of social relationships developed between Englishmen and Indians as a result of a "merging of interests between the two communities" (7). See David Kopf, *British Orientalism and the Bengal Renaissance*. This new spirit is best expressed in a letter by Warren Hastings to Nathaniel Smith, Chairman of the East India Company, in 1784:

> Every accumulation of knowledge and especially such as is obtained by social communication with people over whom we exercise a dominion founded on the right of conquest, is useful to the state . . . it attracts and conciliates distant affections; it lessens the weight of the chain by which the natives are held in subjection; and it imprints on the hearts of our own countrymen the sense and obligation of benevolence.

Quoted in O. P. Kejariwal, *The Asiatic Society of Bengal and the Discovery of India's Past 1784–1838*.

7. Messalina was the wife of Claudius, fourth emperor of Rome. She was put to death for her political crimes and sexual profligacy (*Oxford Classical Dictionary*).

8. See *Shorter Encyclopaedia of Islam* 190 for a brief history of the name.

9. I quote from a conversation between Brandon and his friend Mostyn in which they discuss the relative merits of an Indian and an English wife. Referring to their ancestors, the eighteenth-century Orientalists who had lived happily with Indian wives or concubines, they conclude that even in the present time of racial segregation, an Indian wife had much to recommend her.

10. An epic in Sanskrit which narrates, in the manner of the *Iliad* and the *Odyssey*, the battles, travails, and ultimate destruction of two princely families and their descendants, many of whom are heroes renowned for their martial valor.

11. Gauri Viswanathan, "Currying Favor" 85. An extended version of the argument of this essay is included in her comprehensive *Masks of Conquest*.

12. T. B. Macaulay in his famous minute on Education in India recorded on 2 February 1835 said, "We must at present do our best to form a class of people who may be interpreters between us and the millions whom we govern—a class of persons Indian in blood and colour, but English in tastes, in opinions, in morals and in intellect."

13. Warren Hastings describes the Indians thus in *Excerpts from the evidence of Warren Hastings: Minutes of Evidence before the House of Lords on the East India Company Affairs*, 5 April 1813 (qtd. in Aspinall and Smith 840).

14. The mild, effeminate Hindu was an idea that also dominated legislative history in colonial India, giving rise to the idea of the effeminate 'Bengali babu' who lacked the 'manly' qualities of a good administrator. For an extensive treatment of this subject, see Mrinalini Sinha, *Colonial Masculinity*.

15. The Revolt of 1857 was caused by a complex set of interrelated discontents with the East India Company. It is impossible to summarize all the issues that caused the revolt in different states in North and Central India, but historians agree that both Hindus and Moslems of different classes participated in the uprising. The grievances of the supporters of the rebellion were both economic and cultural. While the native elite were desperate to get back political power and the privileges attached to independent states, the peasants were restless and dissatisfied with the

pressures they had to cope with after the British introduced a new revenue settlement. The Sepoys in the army were angered by rumors that the cartridges they used were greased with cow or pig fat. For outlaws who existed on the peripheries of the law, this was an occasion for plunder and looting. It was thus a complex medley of grievances among many different economic and social constituencies that prompted the armed uprising called the Sepoy Revolt. For different perspectives on the Revolt of 1857 see Ainslee T. Embree's *1857 in India;* William Kaye's *A History of the Sepoy War in India 1857–58;* and Eric Stokes and C. A. Bayly, *The Peasant Armed: the Indian Revolt of 1857.* See also Gautum Chakravarty's *The Indian Mutiny and the British Imagination,* in which he argues that Kaye is thus able to ascribe both the sepoy insurgency and its ultimate containment to the superiority of English administration and its liberal reform of Indian society.

CONCLUSION

1. See Nikita Doval, "Akbar, Jodha to 'romance' again," *The Times of India,* 23 February 2005.
2. For this statement from historian and director of Khuda Baksh Oriental Library in Patna, see Syed Firdaus Ashraf, "Did Jodhabai really exist?" on rediff. com. February 6, 2008.
3. See Sharmishtha Gooptu, "Power of Imagination," *The Times of India.* 23 February 2008.
4. Quoted in Namrata Joshi, "Modern History: A Politically Correct Bollywood Historical Raises Issues Relevant to Our Times," *Outlook India.* March 10, 2008.
5. Quoted in Joshi 1.
6. Gooptu, "Power of Imagination."
7. Syed Firdaus Ashraf points out that Jodhabai is not mentioned in Abul Fazl's *Akbarnama,* Abdul Qadir Badayuni's *Mutakhabutawarikh,* or Nizamuddin Ahmed's *Tabqat-i-Akbari.* See his "Did Jodhabai really exist?"

BIBLIOGRAPHY

UNPUBLISHED SOURCES

Linneaus, William. "Letter to his aunt Mrs. Lostock." 25 May 1815. Gardner Papers. Cambridge South Asia Archive, Cambridge, England.
———. Letters to Edward Gardner. 5 January 1820–23; December 1821. Eur Mss. C 304 Oriental and India Office Collections, London. Transcript in National Army Museum, London. Gardner Papers 6305–56–5.
Kirkpatrick Papers. Eur Mss. F 228/83. India Office Library. British Library, London.

PUBLISHED PRIMARY SOURCES

Diver, Maud. *Lilamani: A Study in Possibilities*. Blackwood, 1920; rpt. Oxford: Oxford University Press, 2004. Ed. Ralph Crane.
———. *The Awakening*. New York: Lane, 1911.
———. *The Dream Prevails*. London: J. Murray, 1938.
Croker, Bithia Mary. *In Old Madras*. Leipzig: Bernhard Tauchnitz, 1913.
———. *Babes in the Wood*. Leipzig: Bernard Tauchnitz, 1910.
———. *The Company's Servant: A Romance of Southern India*. 2 vols. Leipzig: Bernhard Tauchnitz, 1908.
Morgan, Lady (Sydney Owenson). *The Missionary: an Indian tale*. London: J. J. Stockdale, 1811.
Parkes, Fanny. *Wanderings of a Pilgrim in Search of the Picturesque*. 1850; rpt. Karachi and London: Oxford University Press, 1975.
Perrin, Alice. *The Anglo-Indians*. 7th ed. London: Methuen, 1912.

Steel, Flora Annie. *On the Face of the Waters*. London: Heinemann, 1896.
Taylor, Philip Meadows. *The Letters of Philip Meadows Taylor to Henry Reeve*. Ed. Patrick Cadell. London: Oxford University Press, 1947.
———. *A Noble Queen: A Romance of Indian History*. London, 1878.
———. *Ralph Darnell*. London: Kegan, Paul Trench, 1897.
———. *Seeta*. London: Kegan, Paul, Trench, 1887.
———. *Story of My Life*. London: Zwan, 1878; rpt. 1989.
———. *Tara: A Mahratta Tale*. Edinburgh: W. Blackwood, 1863.
———. *Tipoo Sultaun: A Tale of the Mysore War*. London: R. Bentley, 1940.
United Kingdom: Parliament. *Hansard's Parliamentary Debates*. 3rd ser. Vol. 102: 1186.
Wynne, Pamela. *Ann's an Idiot*. London: Philip Allan, 192.
———. *East is always East*. London: Allan, 1930.

PUBLISHED SECONDARY SOURCES

"Adrift in India." *Times Literary Supplement* 21 Feb. 1902, 44.
Ahmed, Siraj. "The Theater of the Civilized Self: Edmund Burke and the East India Trials." *Representations* 78 (Spring 2002): 28–55.
———. "'An Unlimited Intercourse': Historical Contradictions and Imperial Romance in the Early Nineteenth Century." *Romantic Circles Praxis Series: The Containment and Re-Deployment of English India* (2005): 1–27.
Archer, Mildred. *India and British Portraiture 1770–1825*. Delhi: Oxford University Press, 1979.
Armstrong, Nancy. *Desire and Domestic Fiction: A Political History of the Novel*. Oxford: Oxford University Press, 1987.
Arnold, Edwin. *The Marquis of Dalhousie's Administration of British India*. London: Saunders and Otley, 1862.
Ashraf, Syed Firdaus. "Did Jodhabai really exist?" *Refiff.com* Rediff.com., 6 Feb. 20089. Web 23 May, 2008. http://in.rediff.com/cms/print.jsp?docpath=/movies/2008/feb/06jodha.htm. n.pag.
Aspinall, A., and Antony Smith, eds. *English Historical Documents*. London: Eyre and Spottiswoode, 1959.
Bailey, Susan. *Women and the British Empire*. New York: Garland Publishing Company, 1987.
Baird, J. G. A., ed. *Private Letters of the Marquess of Dalhousie*. Edinburgh: Blackwood, 1910.
Ballhatchet, Kenneth. *Race, Sex and Class under the Raj: Imperial Attitudes and Policies and Their Critics, 1793–1905*. London: Weidenfeld and Nicholson, 1980.
Basu, B. D. *The Story of Satara*. Calcutta: Modern Review Office, 1922.
Bayly, C. A. *Empire and Information: Intelligence Gathering and Social Communication in India, 1780–1870*. Cambridge: Cambridge University Press, 1996.
Bearce, George D. *British Attitudes Towards India 1784–1858*. Oxford: Oxford University Press, 1961.
Behl, Aditya. "Articulating a Life, in Words and Pictures: Begum Samru and the Ornament of Histories." *After the Great Mughals: New Light on Eighteenth and Nineteenth Century Painting*. Ed. Barbara Schmitz. Mumbai: Marg Publications, 2002. 100–24.

Benjamin, Walter. "Allegory and Trauerspiel." *The Origin of German Tragic Drama.* Trans. John Osborne. London: Verso, 2003. 159–235.
Brantlinger, Patrick. "Nations and Novels: Disraeli, George Eliot, and Orientalism." *Victorian Studies* (1992): 257–75.
——. *Rule of Darkness: British Literature and Imperialism, 1830–1914.* Ithaca: Cornell University Press, 1988.
Bristow, Joseph. *Empire Boys: Adventure in a Man's World.* London: Harper Collins Academic, 1991.
Brown, Laura. *Ends of Empire: Women and Ideology in Early Eighteenth-Century English Literature.* Ithaca: Cornell University Press, 1993.
Burton, Antoinette. "The White Woman's Burden: British Feminists and 'The Indian Woman,' 1865–1915." *Western Women and Imperialism.* Ed. Nupur Chaudhri and Margaret Strobel. Bloomington: Indiana University Press, 1992. 137–57.
Busia, Abena. "Miscegenation as Metonymy: Sexuality and Power in the Colonial Novel." *Ethnic and Racial Studies* 9.3 (1986): 360–72.
Cadell, Patrick, ed. *The Letters of Philip Meadows Taylor to Henry Reeve.* London: Oxford University Press, 1947.
Chakravarti, Uma. "Whatever Happened to the Vedic *Dasi*? Orientalism, Nationalism and a Script for the Past." *Recasting Women: Essays in Colonial History.* Ed. Kumkum Sangari and Sudesh Vaid. New Delhi: Kali for Women, 1989. 27–87.
Chakravarty, Gautam. *The Indian Mutiny and the British Imagination.* Cambridge: Cambridge University Press, 2005.
Chase, Karen, and Michael Levenson. *The Spectacle of Intimacy: A Public Life for the Victorian Family.* Princeton: Princeton University Press, 2000.
Chatterjee, Indrani. *Gender, Slavery and Law in Colonial India.* Oxford: Oxford University Press, 1999.
Chaudhri, Nupur, and Margaret Strobel, eds. *Western Women and Imperialism: Complicity and Resistance.* Bloomington: Indiana University Press, 1992.
Chowdhry, Prem. "Customs in a Peasant Economy: Women in Colonial Haryana." *Recasting Women: Essays in Colonial History.* Ed. Kumkum Sangari and Sudesh Vaid. New Delhi: Kali for Women, 1989. 302–36.
Copland, Ian. *The British Raj and the Indian Princes: Paramountcy in Western India, 1857–1930.* New Delhi: Orient Longman, 1982.
"Croker, Bithia Mary." *The Feminist Companion to Literature in English: Women Writersw from the Middle Ages to the Present.* Ed. Virginia Blain, Patricia Clements, and Isobel Grundy. New Haven: Yale University Press. 248–49.
Dalrymple, William. *White Mughals: Love and Betrayal in Eighteenth-Century India.* London: Harper, 2002.
David, Deirdre. *Rule Britannia: Women, Empire, and Victorian Writing.* Ithaca: Cornell University Press, 1995.
Davidoff, Leonore, and Catherine Hall. *Family Fortunes: Men and Women of the English Middle Class, 1780–1850.* Chicago: University of Chicago Press, 1987.
Davin, Anna. "Imperialism and Motherhood." *Tensions of Empire: Colonial Cultures in a Bourgeois World.* Ed. Frederick and Ann Stoler Cooper. Berkeley: University of California Press, 1997. 87–151.
De Bruyn, Frans. "Edmund Burke's Gothic Romance: The Portrayal of Warren Hastings in Burke's Writings and Speeches on India." *Criticism* 29.4 (1987): 415–38.

Diver, Maud. *The Awakening*. New York: Lane, 1911.
Donaldson, Laura E. *Decolonizing Feminisms: Race, Gender and Empire Building*. Chapel Hill: University of North Carolina Press, 1992.
Doval, Nikita. "Akbar, Jodha to 'romance' again." *The Times of India*. Indiatimes. com 23 Feb, 1030113,prtpage-1.cms. n.pag.
Dyer, Gary R. "The 'Vanity Fair' of Nineteenth-Century England: Commerce, Women, and the East in the Ladies' Bazaar." *Nineteenth-Century Literature* 46.2 (1991): 196–222.
Elridge, C. C. *England's Mission: The Imperial Idea in the Age of Gladstone and Disraeli, 1868–1880*. London: Macmillan, 1973.
Ellis, Kate Ferguson. *The Contested Castle: Gothic Novls and the Subversion of Domesitc Ideology*. Urbana: University of Illinois Press, 1989.
Embree, Ainslie Thomas, ed. *1857 in India: Mutiny or War of Independence?* Boston: Heath, 1963.
Fisher, Michael. "Becoming and Making 'Family' in Hindustan." *Unfamiliar Relations: Family and History in South Asia*. Ed. Indrani Chatterjee. New Brunswick: Rutgers University Press, 2004. 95–121
———. *Indirect Rule in India: Residents and the Residency System 1764–1858*. Delhi: Oxford University Press, 1991.
———, ed. *The Politics of the British Annexation of India, 1757–1857*. Delhi: Oxford University Press, 1993.
Furber, Holden. "The Theme of Imperialism and Colonialism in Modern Historical Writing on India." *Historians of India, Pakistan, and Ceylon*. Ed. C. H. Philips. London: Oxford University Press, 1961. 332–43.
Gardner, Lionel. *The Sabre and the Spur*. New Delhi: Malhotra, 1985.
"Gardner, William Linnaeus." *The Dictionary of National Biography*. Ed. Leslie Stephen and Sidney Lee. Vol. vii. Oxford: Oxford University Press, 1921–22.
George, Rosemary Marangoly. *The Politics of Home: Postcolonial Relocations and Twentieth-Century Fiction*. Cambridge: Cambridge University Press, 1996.
Ghosh, Durba. *Sex and the Family in Colonial India: The Making of Empire*. Cambridge: Cambridge University Press, 2006.
Ghosh, Suresh Chandra. *Dalhousie in India, 1846–56: A Study of His Social Policy as Governor-General*. Delhi: Munshiram Manoharlal, 1975.
———. *The Social Condition of the British Community in Bengal 1757–1800*. Leiden: Brille, 1970.
Gilman, Sander. "Black Bodies, White Bodies: Towards an Iconography of Female Sexuality in late Nineteenth-Century Art, Medicine, and Literature." *"Race," Writing and Difference*. Ed. Henry Louis Gates. Chicago: University of Chicago Press, 1986. 231–61.
Gooptu, Sharmishtha. "Power of Imagination." *The Times of India*. Indiatimes. com 213 Feb, 2008. Web.21 MaY 2008. http://timesofindia.indiatimes.com/articlesshow/msid-2806120,prtpage-Lems. n.pag.
Greenberger, Allen. *The British Image of India: A Study in the Literature of Imperialism, 1880–1960*. London: Oxford University Press, 1969.
Hammond, N. G. L., and H. H. Scullard. *The Oxford Classical Dictionary*. 2d ed. Oxford: Clarendon, 1970.
Hawes, Clement. *Poor Relations: The Making of a Eurasian Community in British India, 1773–1833*. Richmond, Surry: Curzon, 1996.

Holman, Dennis. *Sikander Sahib: The Life of Colonel James Skinner, 1778–1841*. London: Heinemann, 1961.
Hunt, Lynn Avery. *The Family Romance of the French Revolution*. Berkeley: University of California Press, 1992.
Hunter, William Wilson. *Rulers of India: Marquess of Dalhousie*. Oxford: Clarendon Press, 1895.
Hutchins, Francis. *The Illusion of Permanence: British Imperialism in India*. Princeton, NJ: Princeton University Press, 1967.
Hyam, Ronald. *Empire and Sexuality*. Manchester: Manchester University Press, 1990.
———. "Concubinage and Colonial Service." *Journal of Imperial and Commonwealth History* 14.3 (1986): 170–86.
———. "Empire and Sexual Opportunity." *Journal of Imperial and Commonwealth History* 2 (1986): 35–89.
Inden, Ronald. *Imagining India*. Oxford: Basil Blackwell, 1990.
"Izrael." *Shorter Encyclopedia of Islam*. Ed. H. A. R. Gibbs and J. H. Kramers. Leiden: E. J. Brill, 1953.
Jackson, Charles. *A Vindication of Marquis of Dalhousie's Indian Administration*. Allahabad: Chugh, 1975.
Jameson, Fredric. "Reification and Utopia in Mass Culture." *Social Text* 1 (1979): 130–48.
JanMohamed, Abdul R. "The Economy of Manichean Allegory: The Function of Racial Difference in Colonialist Literature." *Critical Inquiry* 12 (1985): 59–87.
Jerinic, Maria. "How We Lost the Empire: Retelling the Stories of the Rani of Jhansi and Queen Victoria." *Remaking Queen Victoria*. Ed. Margaret Homans and Adrienne Munich. Cambridge: Cambridge University Press, 1997. 123–39.
Johnston, Susan. *Women and Domestic Experience in Victorian Political Fiction*. Westport, CT: Greenwood, 2001.
Jolly, Roslyn. "Stevenson's 'Sterling Domestic Fiction,' *The Beach of Falesá*." *Review of English Studies: A Quarterly Journal of English Literature and the English Language* 50.200 (1999): 463–82.
Joseph, Betty. *Reading the East India Company, 1720–1840: Colonial Currencies of Gender*. Chicago: University of Chicago Press, 2004.
Joshi, Namrata."Modern History: A politically correct Bollywood historical raises issues relevant to our times." *India Outlook Magazine*. Outlookindia.com 10 March, 2008. web 21 May, 2008. http://www.outlookindia.com/article.aspox?236918. n.pag.
Kansteiner, Wulf. "Hayden White's Critique of the Writing of History." *History and Theory* 32.3 (October 1993): 273–95.
Kaye, John William. *A History of the Sepoy War in India 1857–58*. 9th ed. Vol. 1. London: Allen, 1880.
———. *The Administration of the East India Company: A History of Indian Progress*. London: R. Bentley, 1853.
Kejariwal, O. P. *The Asiatic Society of Bengal and the Discovery of India's Past, 1784–1838*. Delhi: Oxford University Press, 1988.
Kopf, David. *British Orientalism and the Bengal Renaissance: The Dynamics of Indian Modernization, 1773–1835*. Berkeley: University of California Press, 1969.
Langbauer, Laurie. *Women and Romance: The Consolations of Gender in the English Novel*. Ithaca: Cornell University Press, 1990.

Langland, Elizabeth. *Nobody's Angels: Middle-Class Women and Domestic Ideology in Victorian Culture.* Ithaca: Cornell University Press, 1995.

Laplanche, Jean, and J. P. Pontalis. *The Language of Psycho-analysis.* New York: Norton, 1973.

Lebra-Chapman, Joyce. *The Rani of Jhansi: A Study in Female Heroism in India.* Honolulu: University of Hawaii Press, 1986.

Lee-Warner, William. *The Protected Princes of India.* London: Macmillan, 1894.

Liggins, Emma, and Daniel Duffy, eds. *Feminist Readings of Victorian Popular Texts: Divergent Femininities.* Aldershot, UK: Ashgate, 2001.

Llewellyn-Jones, Rosie. *A Very Ingenious Man: Claude Martin in Early Colonial India.* Delhi, New York : Oxford University Press, 1992.

Macaulay, Thomas Babington. "Macaulay's Minute." *Selections from Educational Records 1781–1839.* Ed. Henry Sharpe. Calcutta: Superintendent, Government Printing, 1920. 114–18.

Majeed, Javed. "James Mill's *The History of British India* and Utilitarianism as a Rhetoric of Reform." *Modern Asian Studies* 24.2 (1990): 209–24.

———. "Meadows Taylor's *Confessions of a Thug:* The Anglo-Indian Novel as a Genre in the Making." *Writing India 1757–1900.* Ed. Bart Moore-Gilbert. Manchester,: Manchester University Press, 1996. 86–110.

Malchow, H. L. *Gothic Images of Race in Nineteenth-Century Britain.* Stanford: Stanford University Press, 1996.

Malcolm, John. *The Government of India.* London: Murray, 1833.

Mani, Lata. "Contentious Traditions: The Debate on Sati in Colonial India." *Cultural Critique* 7 (1989): 119–56.

———. "The Production of an Official Discourse on Sati in Early Nineteenth-Century Bengal." *Economic and Political Weekly* 31.17 (1986): 32–40.

Marshall, P. J. "The Whites of British India, 1780–1830: A Failed Colonial Society?" *Trade and Conquest: Studies on the Rise of British Dominance in India.* Hampshire: Variorum, 1993. 26–44.

McBratney, John. *Imperial Subjects, Imperial Space: Rudyard Kipling's Fiction of the Native.* Columbus: The Ohio State University Press, 2002.

———. "Lovers beyond the Pale: Images of Indian Women in Kipling's Tales of Miscegenation." *Works and Days* 8.1 [15] (Spring 1990): 17–36.

McLane, John R. *Land and Local Kingship in Eighteenth-Century Bengal.* Cambridge: Cambridge University Press, 1993.

McClintock, Anne. *Imperial Leather: Race, Gender and Sexuality in the Colonial Contest.* New York: Routledge, 1995.

McClure, John. "Late Imperial Romance." *Raritan* 10 (Spring 1991): 111–30.

Mee, Jon. "Austen's Treacherous Ivory: Female Patriotism, Domestic Ideology, and Empire." *The Postcolonial Jane Austen.* Ed. You-me Park and Rajeswari Sunder Rajan. London: Routledge, 2000. 74–91.

Mehta, Uday Singh. *Liberalism and Empire: A Study in Nineteenth-Century British Liberal Thought.* Chicago: University of Chicago Press, 1999.

Melville, Stephen. "Notes on the Re-Emergence of Allegory, the Forgetting of Modernism, the Necessity of Rhetoric, and the Conditions of Publicity in Art and Criticism." *October* 19 (Winter 1981): 55–92.

"Messalina." *The Oxford Classical Dictionary.* 2nd ed. Oxford: Clarendon, 1970.

Meyer, Susan. "Colonialism and the Figurative Strategy of *Jane Eyre.*" *Victorian Studies* 3.2 (1990): 247–68.

———. *Imperialism at Home: Race and Victorian Women's Fiction.* Ithaca: Cornell University Press, 1996.

Mill, John Stuart. *Utilitarianism, Liberty, and Representative Government.* London: Dent, 1910.

Ming, Hanneke. "Barracks Concubinage in the Indies, 1887–1920." *Indonesia* 35 (1983): 65–94.

Mohanty, Satya. "Drawing the Color Line: Kipling and the Culture of Colonial Rule." *The Bounds of Race: Perspectives on Hegemony and Resistance.* Ed. Dominick LaCapra. Ithaca: Cornell University Press, 1991. 311–43.

Mukherjee, Meenakshi. *Realism and Reality: The Novel and Society in India.* New Delhi: Oxford University Press, 1985.

Musselwhite, David. "The Trial of Warren Hastings." *Literature, Politics, and Theory: Papers from the Essex Conference, 1976–84.* Ed. Francis Barker et al. London: Methuen, 1986. 77–103.

Nussbaum, Felicity. *Torrid Zones: Maternity, Sexuality, and Empire in Eighteenth-Century English Narratives.* Baltimore: John's Hopkins University Press, 1995.

Pannikar, K. M. *The Evolution of British Policy towards Indian States, 1774–1858.* Calcutta: Calcutta University Press, 1929.

Papastergiadis, Nikos. "Tracing Hybridity in Theory." *Debating Cultural Hybridity: Multi-cultural Identities and the Politics of Anti-Racism.* Ed. Pnina Werbner and Tariq Madood. London: Zed Books, 1997. 257–81.

Parry, Benita. *Delusions and Discoveries: Studies on India in the British Imagination, 1880–1930.* London: Allen Lane, 1972.

Pasley, Rodney. *Send Malcolm!: A Life of Major General Sir John Malcolm 1769–1833.* London: Basca, 1982.

Paxton, Nancy. *Writing under the Raj: Gender, Race, and Rape in the British Colonial Imagination, 1830–1847.* New Brunswick: Rutgers University Press, 1999.

———. "Secrets of the Colonial Harem: Gender, Sexuality, and the Law in Kipling's Novels." *Writing India 1757–1990: The Literature of British India.* Ed. Bart Moore-Gilbert. Manchester: Manchester University Press, 1996.

———. "Mobilizing Chivalry: Rape in British Novels about the Indian Uprising of 1857." *Victorian Studies* 36.1 (1992 Fall): 5–30.

Perera, Suvendrini. *Reaches of Empire: The English Novel from Edgeworth to Dickens.* New York: Columbia University Press, 1991.

Philips, C. H. "James Mill, Monstuart Elphinstone, and the History of India." *Historians of India, Pakistan, and Ceylon.* Vol. 1. London: Oxford University Press, 1961.

Pihlainen, Kalle. "The Moral of the Historical Story: Textual Differences in Fact and Fiction." *New Literary History* 33 (2002): 39–60.

Poovey, Mary. *Uneven Developments: The Ideological Work of Gender in Mid-Victorian England.* Chicago: University of Chicago Press, 1988.

———. "Ambiguity and Historicism: Interpreting Confessions of a Thug." *Narrative* 12.1 (January 2004): 3–21.

Prasad, Nandan. *Paramountcy under Dalhousie.* Delhi: Ranjit, 1964.

Pure, Simon. "The Londoner." *The Bookman* 52.5 (January 1921): 311–17.

Pykett, Lynn. Afterword. *Beyond Sensation: Mary Elizabeth Braddon in Context.* Ed Marlene Tromp et al. Albany: SUNY Press, 2000.

Radford, Jean. *The Progress of Romance: The Politics of Popular Fiction.* History Workshop Series. Ed. Raphael Samuel. London: Routledge, 1986.

Radway, Janice. *Reading the Romance: Women, Patriarchy, and Popular Literature.* Chapel Hill: University of North Carolina Press, 1984.

Rahim, M. A. *Lord Dalhousie's Administration of the Conquered and Annexed States.* New Delhi: Chand, 1963.

Ramusack, Barbara. "Cultural Missionaries, Maternal Imperialists, Feminist Allies: British Women Activists in India, 1865–1945." *Western Women and Imperialism: Complicity and Resistance.* Ed. Nupur Chaudhri and Margaret Strobel. Bloomington: Indiana University Press, 1992. 119–35.

Ray, Sangeeta. *Engendering India: Woman and Nation in Colonial and Postcolonial Narratives.* Durham: Duke University Press, 2000.

Rocher, Rosane. "British Orientalism in the Eighteenth Century: The Dialectics of Knowledge and Government." *Orientalism and the Postcolonial Predicament.* Ed. Carol Breckenridge and Peter Van der Veer. Philadelphia: University of Philadelphia Press, 1993.

———. "The Early Enchantment of India's Past." *South Asia Review* 8.5 (1984): 1–5.

Roy, Anindyo. *Civility and Empire: Literature and Culture in British India, 1822–1922.* New York: Routledge, 2005.

Roy, Parama. "Discovering India: Imagining *Thuggee.*" *Yale Journal of Criticism* 9.1 (1996): 121–45.

Sabin, Margery. *Dissenters and Mavericks: Writings about India in English, 1765–2000.* Oxford: Oxford University Press, 2002.

———. "The Suttee Romance." *Raritan.* (Fall 1991): 1–24.

Said, Edward. *Culture and Imperialism.* New York: Vintage Books, 1994.

———. *Orientalism.* New York: Vintage Books, 1979.

Sainsbury, Alison. "Married to the Empire: The Anglo-Indian Domestic Novel." *Writing India 1757–1990: The Literature of British India.* Ed. Bart Moore-Gilbert. Manchester: Manchester University Press, 1996. 163–87.

Saksena, Ram Babu. *The Indo-British Poets of Urdu and Persian.* Lucknow: Nawal Kishore Press, 1941.

Samuels, Shirley. *Romances of the Republic: Women, the Family, and Violence in the Literature of the Early American Nation.* New York: Oxford University Press, 1996.

Sangari, Kumkum. "Relating Histories: Definitions of Literacy, Literature, Gender in Nineteenth-Century Calcutta and England." *Rethinking English: Essays in Literature, Language, History.* Ed. Svati Joshi. New Delhi: Trianka, 1991. 32–123.

Sangari, Kumkum, and Sudesh Vaid, eds. *Recasting Women: Essays in Colonial History.* New Delhi: Kali for Women, 1989.

Sen, Sudipta. "Liberal Empire and Illiberal Trade: The Political Economy of 'Responsible Government' in Early British India." *The New Imperial History: Culture, Identity and Modernity in Britain and the Empire 1660–1836.* Cambridge: Cambridge University Press, 2004. 136–54.

Sharpe, Jenny. *Allegories of Empire: The Figure of Woman in the Colonial Text.* Minneapolis: University of Minnesota Press, 1993.

———. "Figures of Colonial Resistance." *Modern Fiction Studies* 35.1 (1989 Spring): 137–55.

Singh, Bhupal. *A Survey of Anglo-Indian Fiction.* London: Curzon, 1974.

Singh, Jyotsna G. *Colonial Narratives, Cultural Dialogues.* New York: Routledge, 1997.

Singha, Radhika. *A Despotism of Law: Crime and Justice in Early Colonial India.* Delhi: Oxford University Press, 1998.

Sinha, Mrinalini. *Colonial Masculinity: The 'Manly Englishman' and the 'Effeminate*

Bengali' in the Late Nineteenth Century. Manchester: Manchester University Press, 1995.

Sollors, Werner. *Interracialism: Black-White Intermarriage in American History, Literature, and Law.* Oxford: Oxford University Press, 2000.

Sommer, Doris. "Allegory and Dialectics: A Match Made in Romance." *Boundary 2* 18.1 (Spring 1991): 60–82.

———. "Irresistible Romance: The Foundational Fictions of Latin America." *Nation and Narration.* Ed. Homi Bhabha. New York: Routledge, 1990. 71–98.

Spear, Percival. "The British Community in Bengal." *Twilight of the Mughals.* Cambridge: Cambridge University Press, 1951. 5–28.

———. *The Nabobs: A Study of the Social Life of the English in Eighteenth-Century India.* London: Oxford University Press, 1963.

Spivak, Gayatri. "The Rani of Sirmur." *History and Theory* 24.3 (1985): 242–72.

———. "Three Women's Texts and a Critique of Imperialism." *"Race," Writing, and Difference.* Ed. Henry Louis Gates Jr. Chicago: University of Chicago Press, 1986. 262–80.

Stallybrass, Peter, and Allon White. *The Politics and Poetics of Transgression.* Ithaca: Cornell University Press, 1989.

Stieg, Margaret. "Indian Romances: Tracts for the Times." *Journal of Popular Culture* 18.4 (1985): 2–15.

Stokes, Eric, and C. A. Bayly. *The Peasant Armed: The Indian Revolt of 1857.* Oxford: Oxford University Press, 1986.

Stoler, Ann Laura. "Sexual Affronts and Racial Frontiers: European Identities and the Cultural Politics of Exclusion in the Colonial Southeast Asia." *Tensions of Empire: Colonial Cultures in a Bourgeois World.* Ed. Frederick Cooper and Ann Laura Stoler. Berkeley: University of California Press, 1997. 199–237.

———. *Race and the Education of Desire: Foucault's History of Sexuality and the Colonial Order of Things.* Durham: Duke University Press, 1995.

———."Carnal Knowledge and Imperial Power: Gender, Race, and Morality in Colonial Asia." *Gender at the Crossroads of Knowledge: Anthropology in the Postmodern Era.* Ed. Micaela di Leonardo. Berkeley: University of California Press, 1991.

———. "Making Empire Respectable: The Politics of Race and Sexual Morality in 20th-Century Colonial Cultures." *Imperial Monkey Business: Racial Supremacy in Social Darwinist Theory and Colonial Practice.* Ed. Jan Breman et al. Amsterdam: Vrije Universiteit University Press, 1990. 35–70.

Suleri, Sara. *The Rhetoric of English India.* Chicago: University of Chicago Press, 1992.

Sunder Rajan, Rajeswari. "'The Shadow of That Expatriated Prince': The Exorbitant Native of *Dombey and Son.*" *Victorian Literature and Culture* 19 (1991): 85–106.

Sutherland, John. Introduction. *The New Nineteenth Century: Feminist Readings of Underread Victorian Fiction.* Ed. Barbara Leah Harman and Susan Meyer. New York: Garland, 1996.

Teltscher, Kate. "Writing Home and Crossing Cultures: George Bogle in Bengal and Tibet, 1770–1775." *A New Imperial History: Culture, Identity and Modernity in Britain and the Empire 1660–1840.* Ed. Kathleen Wilson. Cambridge: Cambridge University Press, 2004. 281–96.

———. *India Inscribed: European and British Writing on India 1600–1800.* New York: Oxford University Press, 1995.

Todd, William B., and Ann Bowden. *Tauchnitz International Editions in English 1841–1955: A Bibliographic History*. New York: Bibliographic Society of America, 1988.
Travers, Robert. *Ideology and Empire in Eighteenth-Century India*. Cambridge: Cambridge University Press, 2007.
Trotter, L. J. *The Marquis of Dalhousie*. London: Allen, 1889.
Tuite, Clara. "Domestic Retrenchment and Imperial Expansion." *The Postcolonial Jane Austen*. Ed. You-me Park and Rajeswari Sunder Rajan. London: Routledge, 2000. 93–115.
Vèrges, Françoise. *Monsters and Revolutionaries: Colonial Family Romance and Metissage*. Durham: Duke University Press, 1999.
Viswanathan, Gauri. "The Beginnings of English Literary Study in British India." *Oxford Literary Review* 9.1–2 (1987): 2–26.
———. "Currying Favor: The Politics of British Educational and Cultural Policy in India, 1813–1854." *Social Text* 19–20 (1988): 85–104.
———. *Masks of Conquest: Literary Study and British Rule in India*. New York: Columbia University Press, 1989.
———. "Raymond Williams and British Colonialism." *Yale Journal of Criticism* 4.2 (1991): 47–66.
White, Hayden. *Tropics of Discourse: Essays in Cultural Criticism*. Baltimore: Johns Hopkins University Press, 1978.
Wilson, Kathleen. *A New Imperial History: Culture, Identity, and Modernity in Britain and the Empire, 1660–1840*. Ed. Kathleen Wilson. New York: Cambridge University Press, 2004.
Wolff, Robert Lee. *Nineteenth-Century Fiction: A Bibliographic Catalogue Based on the Collection Formed by Robert Lee Wolff*. Vol. 1. New Jersey: Garland, 1981.
Young, Robert. *Colonial Desire: Hybridity in Theory, Culture and Race*. London: Routledge, 1995.
Zastoupil, Lynn. *John Stuart Mill and India*. Stanford: Stanford University Press, 1994.

INDEX

Ahmed, Siraj, 9, 138nn23–24
Arnold, Edwin, 144n1
Ashraf, Syed Firdaus, 147n2, 147n7
Akbar, 131, 132, 133, 147n1
Anglo-Indians, The, 54,
Anglo-Indian, 29, 31; 42; culture, 6, 9, 17, 19–21, 32, 142n3; definition of, 135n4; domesticity, 144n3; fiction, 142n8; novel, 145n3, 52; relations, 29, 40; romance, 2–3, 4–17, 19, 31, 133, 143n13; society, 59, 62, 63, 73, 125, 129; writers, 37
allegory: political, 2, 3, 15, 85, 108; 123, 133; literary, 19–21
annexations: 17, 18, 79, 81,82, 83, 86, 87, 88, 92; Jhansi, 18, 83, 86, 92, 104–7; Nagpur, 97–102; Sambalpur, 102–4; Satara, 92–96
Archer, Mildred, 1, 25, 29, 30, 136n12, 139n2, 139n5
Armstrong, Nancy, 76

Ballhatchet, Kenneth, 136n12, 139n1, 140n13

Basu, B. D., 93, 94, 95, 96, 144n1
Behl, Aditya, 141n14
Benjamin, Walter, 20–21
Brantlinger, Patrick, 141n1, 145n3
Brown, Laura, 136n6
Burke, Edmund, 12, 80, 91, 138n23, 138n24
Burton, Antoinette, 142n3
Boulone. *See* Martin, Claude
Busia, Abena, 142n6

Chakravarti, Uma, 137n20, 138n22
Chakravarty, Gautam, 147n15
Chase, Karen, 137n18
Chatterjee, Indrani, 5, 98, 136nn9–10
Chowdhry, Prem, 145n7
Colebrook, Henry, 11, 138n22
Copland, Ian, 83–84, 143n5
Cornwallis, Governor-General, 89, 98, 143n5
Crewe, Lord, 29
Croker, Bithia Mary, 17, 31–32, 52–77 passim; Works: *Beyond the Pale,* 56; *The Cat's Paw,* 56; *The Company's Servant,* 53, 70–72; *In*

Old Madras, 53. See also *In Old Madras*

Gowariker, Ashutosh, 131
Greenberger, Allan, 57

Dalhousie, Lord, 80, 83, 88, 95–102 passim, 105, 143n5, 143n6, 144n1, 145n11
Dalrymple, William, 35, 36, 37, 46, 48, 128–30, 141n4, 141n7, 141nn13–14
David, Dierdre, 9, 141n1
Diver, Maud, 4, 5, 16
domesticity: Anglo-Indian 6, 59–61, 76, 142n3; and class, 59, 66, 75; ideology of, 4–5, 9; 57–58, 76–77; Indian, 64, 82, 115, interracial, 2, 6, 15–17, 24, 52, 65, 70, 72, 73, 120, 128–30; and politics, 9, 82, 115, realism and, 6; Victorian, 4–6, 54
Doval, Nikita, 147n1
Duffy, Daniel, 54, 76
Dyer, Gary R., 143n14

Ellis, Kate, 64
Embree, Ainslee, 147n15
Eurasian, 28–29, 41, 48, 57, 58, 61, 64, 66, 68, 135n4, 140n13, 140n14

Fisher, Michael, 82, 84, 87, 105, 141n14, 144n7, 145n11

Gardner, Lionel, 36, 141n5
Gardner, William Linneaus, 16, 17, 31, 33–51 passim; chivalry, 37–38, 49; cultural syncretism, 41–42, 44–48, 51; Gardner's Horse, 24, 35; relationship with his son, 48–49; relationship with his wife, 33–34, 37, 38–40, 43, 49–50
George, Rosemary, 5, 142n3
Ghosh, Durba, 6–7, 24–25, 139n4, 140n15
Ghosh, S. C., 29, 139n3, 140nn10–11
Gooptu, Sharmishta, 133, 147n3, 147n6

Hastings, Warren, 12, 24, 28, 89, 91, 111, 121, 137n19, 138n23, 146n6, 146n13
Hastings, Marquess of, 36
Hawes, Clement, 140n14
Heart of Darkness (Conrad), 8, 70, 74, 142n2, 142n6
Holman, Dennis, 139n6
Houston, Gail Turley, 143n15
Hunt, Lynn, 14, 139n26
Hyam, Ronald, 29, 110, 140n13

Impey, Elijah, 90–91
indirect rule, 3, 5, 12, 17, 18, 79–85, 88, 89, 90, 92–107 passim, 112–16, 144n7
In Old Madras (Croker), bazaar, 56, 60, 64, 68–69, 143n14; domestic novel, 52, 54, 76, 142n3, 143n13; gothic, 64, 70, 76; maiming of Englishman, 73–74. See also domesticity and Anglo-Indian, interracial

Jackson, Charles, 97–98, 99–101, 144n1
Jerinic, Maria, 9, 104–5
Jhansi, Rani of, 9, 12, 87–88, 104–7, 145n12
Jodha Akbar, 131–33
Jodha, 131, 132, 133, 147nn1–2, 147n7
Johnson-Woods, Toni, 143n15
Jolly, Roslyn, 141n11, 142n2
Jones, William, 11, 137n19
Joseph, Betty, 13, 90, 145n6
Joshi, Namrata, 147nn4–5

Kansteiner, Wulf, 139n29
Kaur, Amber, 24, 25, 26
Kaye, J. W., 144n1, 147n15
Kim (Kipling), 41, 69

Kipling, Rudyard, 4, 41, 53, 55, 57, 69, 109, 135n5, 137n14
Kirkpatrick, James Achilles, 16, 24, 35, 36, 37, 39–40, 45, 48, 128–30, 141n8, 141n10
Kejariwal, O. P., 146n6
Kopf, David, 137n19, 140n12, 145n6

Langland, Elizabeth, 136n8,
Laplanche, Jean, 135n3
Levenson, Michael. See Chase, Karen.
Lebra-Chapman, Joyce, 106, 145n12
Lee-Warner, William, 83, 89, 98, 144n1
liberal: imagination, 2, 3; 12, 107; 108, 119, 125; politics, 14, 15, 21, 79–82, 84, 100, 107, 125, 127, 131, 143n4, 147n15
Liggins, Emma, 54, 76
Lilamani (Diver), 4, 16, 54

Mah Munzalool nissa, Begum, 17, 33, 36, 33–51 passim. See also Gardner, William Linneaus
Malcolm, John, 81–82
Malet, Charles Warre, 24, 25
Mani, Lata, 7, 138n21, 143n3, 144n5
Martin, Claude, 1–3, 16
McBratney, John, 9, 41, 135n5, 137n14
McLane, John R., 136n10
Mehta, Uday, 81
Melville, Stephen, 21
Meyer, Susan, 137n16, 141n1
Mill, James, 11
Mill, John Stuart, 80–81
Mutiny of 1857, 12, 29, 53, 79, 84, 86, 87, 104, 106, 122, 146n15

Nusbaum, Felicity, 136n6

orientalist: idealization of women, 4, 11, 119–20, 137n13, 138n20; learning, 28,108, 110, 111, 117, 120, 124, 125, 137n18, 140n12, 145n6; romance,16, 38, 146n9
Owenson, Sydney, 16

Palmer, William, 24, 111
Papastergiadis, Nikos, 140n18
Parkes, Fanny, 38, 39, 43, 44, 46, 50
Paxton, Nancy, 9, 53, 106, 136n13, 142nn3–4
Pihlainen, Kalle, 19, 139n30
Pontalis, J. B. See Laplanche, Jean
Poovey, Mary, 136n8, 145n3
Prasad, Nandan, 143n6
Puri, Stine Simonsen, 133
Pykett, Lynn, 143n15

Rahim, M. A., 87, 96, 97, 99, 100, 101, 102, 103, 144n1, 145n9
Ramusack, Barbara, 142n3
Reeve, Henry, 108, 112, 145n2
Resident: dealings with native states: Satara, 93–96; Nagpur, 97–102; Sambalpur, 103, 105, 107; position and responsibilities, 84–86, 88, 144n7; of states: Delhi, 44; Hyderabad, 24, 81,128, 130; Nepal, 34; Poona, 24; and widows, 82, 86–88, 108
Roy, Anidyo, 10
Roy, Parama, 9, 145n3

Sabin, Margery, 11–12
Sainsbury, Allison, 54, 76, 142n3, 142n7, 143n13
Saksena, Ram Babu, 50, 51, 141n16
Samru, Begum, 44–45, 87, 141n14
Samuels, Shirley, 136n6
Sangari, Kumkum, 119
Sati, 7, 11, 12, 13, 33, 89, 122, 138n21, 138n22, 139n28, 142n4, 144n5
Scott, Walter, 109, 121
Seeta (Taylor): education of Indians, 119–20, 125, 126, 146n12; interracial marriage, 110, 111, 120,

123–25; representation of Indians, 118–19, 121–23, 126; See also Mutiny of 1857; Orientalist
Sen, Sudipta, 80, 143n4
Sharpe, Jenny, 9, 30, 136n13, 137n16, 141n1
Shikoh, Suleiman, 50–52
Shorapur, Rani of, 108–9, 112–16, 127
Singh, Bhupal, 54, 142n8
Singh, Jyotsna, 16, 139n27
Sinha, Mrinalini, 143n3, 146n14
Skinner, James, 26–27, 42, 139n6
Sommer, Doris, 19–20, 21, 133
Spear, Perceval, 27, 140nn8–9, 140n17
Spivak, Gayatri, 7, 8, 9, 13, 16, 137n15, 139n28, 141n1
Steel, Flora Annie, 3, 5, 55, 64
Stieg, Margaret, 54, 142n3, 142n7
Stokes, Eric, 147n15
Stoler, Ann Laura, 6, 57–58, 136n11, 143n12
Suleri, Sara, 9, 10, 138n23, 138n25
Sunder Rajan, Rajeswari, 141n1
Sutherland, John, 143n15

Taylor, Philip Meadows, 16, 18, 55, 80, 85, 108–27 passim; relationship with the Rani of Shorapur, 18, 85, 108, 111, 112–16, 127; Orientalist ideas, 111, 125; Works: *The Letters of Philip Meadows Taylor to Henry Reeve*, 108, 122; *A Noble Queen: A Romance of Indian History*, 109; *Ralph Darnell*, 109; *Seeta; Story of My Life; Tara: A Mahratta Tale*, 109; *Tipoo Sultan: A Tale of the Mysore War*, 109. See also *Seeta*; Shorapur, Rani of
Teltscher, Kate, 34, 137n13
Travers, Robert, 89, 91, 144nn2–3, 144n4
Tuite, Clara, 8

Vèrges, Françoise, 14–15
Victoria, Queen, 9, 105, 143n5
Viswanathan, Gauri, 119, 143n3, 146n11
Viswanathan, Shiv, 133

Wellesley, Lord, 36, 39, 82, 129, 130, 143n5
White, Hayden, 18–19, 139nn29–30
White Mughals (Dalrymple), 35, 45–46, 128–29, 141n4
Williamson, Thomas, 26, 139n5
Wilson, Kathleen, 137n17
Wombwell, John, 24, 25
Wynne, Pamela, 54

Young, Robert, 7–8, 141n12

Zastoupil, Lynn, 81

VICTORIAN CRITICAL INTERVENTIONS
Donald E. Hall, Series Editor

Included in this series are provocative, theory-based forays into some of the most heated discussions in Victorian studies today, with the goal of redefining what we both know and do in this field.

*The Affective Life of the Average Man:
The Victorian Novel and the Stock-Market Graph*
Audrey Jaffe

Lost Causes: Historical Consciousness in Victorian Literature
Jason B. Jones

Problem Novels: Victorian Fiction Theorizes the Sensational Self
Anna Maria Jones

Detecting the Nation: Fictions of Detection and the Imperial Venture
Caroline Reitz

*Novel Professions: Interested Disinterest and the Making
of the Professional in the Victorian Novel*
Jennifer Ruth

*Perspectives: Modes of Viewing and Knowing
in Nineteenth-Century England*
Linda M. Shires

*Performing the Victorian: John Ruskin and Identity in Theater,
Science, and Education*
Sharon Aronosky Weltman

The Old Story, with a Difference: Pickwick's Vision
Julian Wolfreys

www.ingramcontent.com/pod-product-compliance
Lightning Source LLC
Chambersburg PA
CBHW020949230426
43666CB00005B/243